Humanizing Information Technology

Julian Warner

The Scarecrow Press, Inc.
Lanham, Maryland, and Oxford
2004

SCARECROW PRESS, INC.

Published in the United States of America
by Scarecrow Press, Inc.
A wholly owned subsidiary of
The Rowman & Littlefield Publishing Group, Inc.
4501 Forbes Boulevard, Suite 200, Lanham, Maryland 20706
www.scarecrowpress.com

PO Box 317
Oxford
OX2 9RU, UK

British Library Cataloguing in Publication Information Available

Library of Congress Cataloging-in-Publication Data

Warner, Julian, 1955–
Humanizing information technology / Julian Warner.
p. cm.
Includes bibliographical references and index.
ISBN: 978-0-8108-4956-3
1. Information science. 2. Information technology—Social aspects.
3. Information society. 4. Information storage and retrieval systems.
I. Title.
Z665 .W27 2004
303.48'33—dc22 2003017048

™ The paper used in this publication meets the minimum requirements of American National Standard for Information Sciences—Permanence of Paper for Printed Library Materials, ANSI/NISO Z39.48-1992.
Manufactured in the United States of America.

Contents

List of Figures

Preface

Humanizing Information Technology develops a dialogue between a stress on the autonomy of information and the determining power of economic base. The ideas of information as an autonomous variable and of the primacy of theoretical knowledge have been recurrent themes in discussions of the information society. A contrasting perspective, associated, although not exclusively, with Marx, would regard existence as producing consciousness, including information and theoretical knowledge. In view of the significance of the contrasting perspective, and of the wide currency of the information society concept, it is surprising that there have not been more deliberate attempts at this dialogue.

Empirical and historical studies are conducted in a dialectic with the theoretical view developed of information technology as a human construction. The chapters progress from outlining the theoretical perspective; to topics studied from, and developing, this perspective; to an anticipation of future developments, including situating information science in relation to contiguous disciplines.

The opening chapter, "An Information View of History," develops a manifesto for the study of information technologies in human history. The proposed study is further developed by, "Organs of the Human Brain, Created by the Human Hand: Towards an Understanding of Information Technology." A move is made toward a synthesis of the primacy of theoretical knowledge and the determining power of the economic base. Technology is fully recognized as a human construction and knowledge is understood as a social relation between men.

"Information Society or Cash Nexus? A Study of the United States as a Copyright Haven" is a theoretically informed historical study, concerned with the autonomy of information. It also serves to bring an episode that has been subject to collective forgetting or repression back to modern consciousness.

In "As Sharp as a Pen: Direct Semantic Ratification in Oral, Written, and Electronic Communication," electronic communication is understood from the historical perspective of oral and written communication. The influence of technology on human conduct is recognized, while technological determinism is avoided, by admitting the possibility of reciprocal interaction between information technologies and the social conditions that produced those technologies.

"In the Catalogue Ye Go for Men: Evaluation Criteria for Information Retrieval Systems" brings a historical perspective on information retrieval to inform understanding of current developments. A design principle for information retrieval systems of an enhanced capacity for informed choice is advocated. The principle is closer to ordinary discourse understandings, as well as to historical precedents, than the dominant modern concern with the transformation of a query into results. "Meta- and Object-Language for Information Retrieval Research: Proposal for a Distinction" addresses the conceptual confusion of information retrieval research and proposes a more rigorous distinction between discussions of information retrieval systems and the transformations possible within such systems.

"Forms of Labor in Information System" looks at the labor involved in information systems. A dynamic involving the substitution of dead for living labor is detected. Developments in information retrieval systems and copyright are then considered, recombining theoretical and empirical contexts. Finally, "W(h)ither Information Science?" is concerned with isolating and carrying forward valuable elements in information science.

A humanistic and historical perspective on information and information and information technologies is offered to communities beyond information science. This book also cumulates and give coherence to work, while readdressing the information science community (some of the chapters have been published as journal articles or delivered as oral conference presentations within information science).

The book, compared to the journal article, is customarily a dialogic form, inviting reviews. The value of the intellectual (and physical) labor embodied in this book, and in the dialogue it may generate, lies in developing an understanding of the conditions under which we make our own history and of the possibility of influencing our future history.

Acknowledgments

I would like to thank Aslib: the Association for Information Management for permission to adapt articles published by them.

"Chapter 2: Organs of the Human Brain, Created by the Human Hand: Toward an Understanding of Information Technology" is a republication, with slight editorial alterations, of Julian Warner. "What Should We Understand By Information Technology (And Some Hints At Other Issues)?" *Aslib Proceedings*. 52, 9, 2000, 350-370.

"Chapter 5: In The Catalogue Ye Go For Men: Evaluation Criteria for Information Retrieval Systems" was also published in *Aslib Proceedings*. 52, 2, 2000, 76-82.

I would like to thank John Wiley & Sons, Inc. for permission to reprint the article "Chapter 3: Information Society or Cash Nexus? A Study of the United States as a Copyright Haven," originally published in the *Journal of the American Society for Information Science*. 50, 5, 1999, 461-470. © John Wiley & Sons, Inc. 1999.

I would like to thank the University of Chicago Press for permission to reprint the article "Chapter 8: W(h)ither Information Science?," originally published as Julian Warner. "W(h)ither Information Science?/!" *Library Quarterly*. 71, 2, 2001, 243-255. © University of Chicago Press.

I would also like to acknowledge the American Society for Information Science and Technology.

A version of "Chapter 4: As Sharp as a Pen: Direct Semantic Ratification in Oral, Written, and Electronic Communication" was given as an oral presentation to the Annual Conference of the American Society for Information Science, Washington, D.C., November 2001.

I would also like to thank Elisabeth Davenport and Boyd Rayward for encouragement and advice.

Chapter 1

An Information View of History

The concept of the information society, associated, for instance, with Daniel Bell (D. Bell, 1980) has been subjected to increasingly severe critiques. The ideas of a sharp disjunction with pre-existing forms of social organization and of information as an autonomous or determining variable, and the lack of historical perspective in the information society concept, have all been criticized (Finnegan, 1989; Webster, 1995a). A productive counterproposal of the informatization of social life, which acknowledges the increased significance of information to the modern world but that also stresses historical continuities, has begun to be developed (Webster, 1995a).

A further adaptation of the information society concept can be proposed: an information view of history. A revealing historical analogy to this perspective on history can be made. Marx (1976) and Darwin (1968) tended to see evolution and human history as struggle or competition, with particular emphasis on physical control over the environment. Now as information technologies are further developed and comprehended by the generic term *information technology*, human history can be studied to reveal the development of means of communication.

The possibility of the historical study of technologies was opened up by Marx in *Capital*, although with reference to forms of technology concerned with the human transformation of the material environment.

> A critical history of technology would show how little any of the inventions of the eighteenth century are the work of a single individual. As yet such a book does not exist. Darwin has directed attention to the history of natural technology, i.e. the formation of the organs of plants and animals, which serve as the instruments of production for sustaining their life. Does not the history of the productive organs of man in society, of organs that are the material basis of every particular organization of society, deserve equal attention? And would not such a history be easier to compile, since,

> as Vico says, human history differs from natural history in that we have made the former, but not the latter? (Marx, 1976, 493-494)

The application of this approach to information technologies would be a task for our time.

In the *Grundrisse*, a similar, and more explicit, view of technology as a human construction had been developed.

> Nature builds no machines, no locomotives, railways, electric telegraphs, self-acting mules etc. These are products of human industry; natural material transformed into organs of the human will over nature, or of or human participation in nature. They are *organs of the human brain, created by the human hand*; the power of knowledge objectified. (Marx, 1973a, 706)

From this basis, a modern understanding of technology as a special form of knowledge dealing with the transformation of the material environment into useful goods and services has been developed, particularly by Nathan Rosenberg (N. Rosenberg, 1976, 1982, 1994). The obdurate materiality of the machine is still recognized as essential to its social function (MacKenzie, 1996). Some critical distinctions are made: invention is distinguished from innovation, or the adoption of the invented product, and diffusion mechanisms and path-dependency, the strong influence of early events on subsequent developments, are recognized. On this model, information technology could be regarded as a form of knowledge concerned with the transformation of signals from one form or medium into another, with the other crucial distinctions retained.

Information science could then contribute a greater and more specific historical perspective on information technologies and on the informatization of life than is generally encountered. For instance, a distinction between invention and innovation can be discovered in the development of copyright. Information technologies, from telegraphic codes to computer programs, have to be adopted and reach certain levels of social significance before they impinge on the judiciary or legislature (Warner, 1993a). In the gap between first announcement, possibly to claim scientific priority, and judicial, and even more legislative, response, a distinction between invention and innovation is embodied. It can be retrieved with a high degree of historical specificity. Preliminary evidence from the admission of nonbook media to copyright protection by legislation (Warner, 1993a) indicates that the late nineteenth century in the United States was as a (if not *the*) critical period for the adoption of interconnected information technology innovations (Beniger, 1986; see chapter 2). The period has been characterized as the age of invention (Bryson, 1998) and the question, Why in America? addressed, with regard to technologies for transforming natural resources (Rosenberg, 1994). If the same question were asked for information technologies, it could be responded that similar conditions for hospitality to innovation applied, but that, in addition, continental expansion and increasing links with Europe demanded technologies for the rapid communication of messages over space (see chapter 2). The rapid adoption of the telephone and the telegraph, the transformation of invention into innovation, can be understood in this context.

In conclusion, an information view of history can be developed that would benefit information science and other communities interested in the informatization of life. For information science, the unreflexiveness of its response to information technology developments can be diminished, and, to other communities, a historically specific but also theoretically informed view of information technologies can be offered.

Chapter 2

Organs of the Human Brain, Created by the Human Hand: Toward an Understanding of Information Technology

From the thesis that being or social existence determines consciousness, the set of activities labeled as information science (Roberts, 1976) have been convincingly regarded as a partly unreflexive response to post-1945 developments in computer and telecommunications technology (Brown, 1987, 113-115; V. Rosenberg, 1974). Specifically, information science has been understood as part of a pattern in which "New tools beget new sciences" (Brown, 1987, 115). Yet information science has had a limited understanding of information technology and could be regarded as having repressed or disguised its origins.

The understanding of information technology has been limited in a number of ways, often by implication rather than by explicit statement. Information technology may be regarded as objectively given or an autonomous development, particularly as implied by the language of discussion (Levinson, 1997; Warner, 1998b). There are also traces of technological determinism, most subtly and pervasively in the limited recognition of information technology as a human construction (Hancock-Beaulieu, 1992; Kahin and Nesson, 1997; Warner, 1993b; 1998a). Historical consciousness has also been limited and the crucial question of the critical period for the development of modern information technologies has only been briefly addressed (see chapter 1). The positions implied, and here identified, may not reach the level of formal articulation and can appear weak when articulated. A specific feature of repression would be to claim to focus on information processes but then to allow topics for investigation to be largely determined by the potentialities of current information technologies. These assertions would admit of qualification, particularly with regard to the growth of historical consciousness, and have been partly eroded by recent contributions but still characterize the dominant tenor of the field.

There are some analogies with extradisciplinary perspectives, that may have also influenced intradisciplinary thought. A strong, although largely implicit, analogy with the reception of technology as objectively given would be with the, often dominant, Platonist view of mathematical propositions as discovered rather than humanly created. This may have unconsciously, but still powerfully, influenced the thinking of information scientists from mathematical and scientific backgrounds (Roberts, 1976). More broadly, there has been a divide of technical from social and human thought: crudely put, technology has been left to the technicians, who may not be concerned with issues of human and social significance (Wyn and Katz, 1997); and one strong humanist attitude has been to regard technology as something artificial, a perspective plausibly inherited from responses to industrial technology. The linguistic resources of public discourse remain inadequate to understanding current technology (Gilfillan, 1970; Winner, 1977, 2-11). An unexplored sociotechnical dynamic persists (Walsham, 1998, 1087).

The limited understanding of information technology in information science is unfortunate, in two major respects. It restricts its understanding of itself, of its historical development, and the historical circumstances that produced it. It also limits its contribution to other disciplines and to wider public discourse, although there are elements in information science, and in contiguous and contributing areas of study, that could contribute to a theoretically sophisticated and historically specific understanding of information technology.

The aim here is to begin the task of articulating a counterposition to the limited understanding of information technology in information science. Drawing on a contributing and partly contiguous discipline, on theoretical computer science, the conception of the computer as a machine will be expanded to encompass other information technologies. The concept of "technology," elided in the understanding of the computer as a machine, will be reinvigorated by drawing on an understanding of technology as a human construction, derived from Marx and largely mediated by economics. The further developments envisaged on the basis of the understanding of information technology established will be briefly foreshadowed: the series of systematic distinctions, from invention, through innovation, to diffusion, which can be used to explore the sociotechnical dynamic, will be introduced; evidence for the late-nineteenth-century United States as the critical period for the development of modern information technologies will be reviewed; and the question of why these technologies should have been produced at that time and in that place will be addressed.

Computer as a Machine

A sophisticated discussion of the computer as machine is offered by Marvin Minsky (1967). In this context, it is valuable both for distinctions made and for distinctions implied, with a continuum between these.

The most crucial distinction is explicitly made in a differentiation of the computer from productive technology. The computer does not

> do "work" as did machines of the Industrial Revolution. Instead of dealing with material or energy . . . they handle "control" and "information." (Minsky, 1967, vii)

Minsky himself notes that the classical idea of a simple machine, such as a lever, wheel, or inclined plane, only helps understand the transmission of force and not the control mechanisms within such machines, such as the ratchet (Minsky, 1967, 7). The distinction from productive technology, and the concern of the computer with transforming information, has been accepted in computer science, at the level of a grounding assumption. The proposal here, which should be equally readily acceptable, is explicitly to extend this distinction and conception to other information technologies. At the initial level of analysis, no distinction is made between technologies used in human communication and control mechanisms within machines, and, for some purposes, this would be a valuable further distinction.

The image of the machine is also considered. The use of term *machine* in ordinary discourse does not evoke a sympathetic object:

> It brings to mind a big, heavy, complicated object which is noisy, greasy, and metallic; performs jerky, repetitive, and monotonous motions; and has sharp edges that may hurt one if he does not maintain sufficient distance. (Minsky, 1967, 1)

Notions of mechanism and determinism may be simultaneously evoked (Minsky, 1967, 1). The implication of an inheritance from and continuity with attitudes to industrial technologies can be briefly contextualized. For instance, Charles Dickens in *Hard Times* was said to view Coketown and its industrial machinery "as a slightly disgusted Southern visitor would see it" (Orwell, 1946, 48). Similarly, Norbert Wiener comments on the image of the shed factory as "one of the crueler circles of the hell of the Industrial Revolution" (Wiener, 1993, 93). The unsympathetic image of the machine may partly account for the reluctance to acknowledge technology as a human construction. In addition, the association of both productive and information technology with mechanism and determinism might further explain the humanistic resistance to technology, currently being eroded (see chapter 8).

A further description of the computer offered by Minsky, as a strange new species (Minsky, 1967, viii), is more valuable for what it implies or reveals than what it explicitly states. It anticipates the widely promulgated view of the computer as a "radical novelty" (Dijkstra, 1989; Leith, 1990; Warner, 1994). In this context, it can be regarded as an unconscious reproduction of the innovatory dynamism of capitalism, with its revolutionary rather than conservative technical base (Marx, 1976, 617). It also obscures the human labor involved in the production of the computer, and, as has been more widely recognized, its historical antecedents in other information technologies (Leith, 1990). At the level of specific historical events, rather than theoretical understanding, Minsky recognizes the historical development of the theory of computation and of the computer and questions the received view of a divorce between seminal papers in mathematical logic in the 1930s and the construction of working computers (Minsky, 1967, 104). The received view does reinforce the separation between the understanding of the possibilities and limits of computation and of the computer as a form of technology.

The aim of the investigation and exposition of the computational process is, for Minsky, to develop a grasp of fundamental matters and bring this understanding back to the practical world (Minsky, 1967, 2-3). With some exceptions, the challenge to return to the practical world has not been accepted and automata studies has been pursued as an autonomous activity, with a curious combination of restrained theory and mystical practice observed (Leith, 1990), and, possibly, resulting (Warner, 1994). The proposal here is to extend the differentiation of the computer from industrial machines, as being concerned with the transformation of information inputs into information outputs, to other information technologies, and to reinvigorate the understanding of technology.

Understandings of Technology

The classic source for an understanding of technology as a human construction is Marx, although his work has been subject to neglect and distortion (Buhle, 1991; Haye, 1980, 10). Since the early 1990s, Marxism has become intensely unfashionable (Mackenzie, 1996, 18). For earlier periods, it has been convincingly suggested that the strong polemical orientation associated with Marxist studies limited the diffusion of its treatment of technology (N. Rosenberg, 1976, 126). A misleading view of Marx as technological determinist did, however, gain sufficient credence to be worthy of repudiation (Mackenzie, 1996, 23-46). Marx's views on technology have been largely mediated by economics, particularly by Rosenberg (N. Rosenberg, 1976; 1982; 1994), and although information technologies, such as the telegraph, have been studied (Rosenberg, N., 1994, 203-231), the issue of their differentiation from productive technologies has not been explicitly addressed. With the exceptions of Wiener, who both by explicit allusions and thematic echoes reveals an acquaintance with Marxist thought (Wiener, 1954, 4; 1993), and, more obviously and polemically, J. D. Bernal, there has only been a limited penetration of Marxism into information science. Yet, as in economics, with its primary focus on productive technologies, a Marxian perspective on information technology could be of high marginal utility.

The social construction of technology movement is better, although not fully, known within information science, particularly through recent imports (Kling, Rosenbaum, and Hert, 1998). A comparative reading would suggest that it has developed partly, although not entirely, separately from the Marxian approach mediated by economics, and is not necessarily fully aware of potentially relevant antecedents. Its focus has been on computer technologies, and, within that, on software rather than on the computer as a machine. To some extent, it has also emphasized the social shaping rather than the radical human construction of technologies (Stewart and Williams, 1998). The Marxian approach promises to be richer and fuller, although, as yet, less fully developed, inclusive of productive and other information technologies, of the computer as a machine as well as software, and emphasizing the human construction as well as the social shaping of technologies. The intersection, or lack of intersection, between the Marxian approach mediated by economics and the social construction of technology movement could form a focus for further study, possibly supported by bibliometric methods, with a view to their mutual synthesis.

A view of technology as human construction is given by a classic passage in the *Grundrisse*:

> Nature builds no machines, no locomotives, railways, electric telegraphs, self-acting mules etc. These are products of human industry; natural material transformed into organs of the human will over nature, or of human participation in nature. They are *organs of the human brain, created by the human hand*; the power of knowledge objectified. The development of fixed capital indicates to what degree general social knowledge has become a *direct force of production*, and to what degree, hence, the conditions of the process of social life itself have come under control of the general intellect and been transformed in accordance with it. To what degree the powers of social production have been produced, not only in the form of knowledge, but also as immediate organs of social practice, of the real life process. (Marx, 1973a, 706)

In accord with the tenor of the industrial age (see also chapter 7), the primary emphasis of this passage is on technology as a means for transforming the material environment, and, although transport and information technologies (both for human communication and machine control) are cited, they are not explicitly differentiated.

Some further aspects of the passage deserve comment. The crucial distinction, which guides Marx's treatment of technology, is made between natural developments and human products. From this perspective, even domestic animals would be regarded as a form of technology as they been deliberately modified by human intellectual and physical labor, *malgré eux* (Marx, 1976, 285). Knowledge as social practice is distinguished from knowledge in itself. In the reference to the "general intellect," there is an anticipation of categories later explicitly introduced in the third volume of *Capital*, of universal and communal human labor:

> They both play their part in the production process, and merge into one another, but they are each different as well. Universal labour is all sci-

> entific work, all discovery and invention. It is brought about partly by the cooperation of men now living, but partly also by building on earlier work. Communal labour, however, simply involves the direct cooperation of individuals. (Marx, 1981, 199)

The distinction can be discovered in domains familiar to information science: patent rights could be regarded a restriction on the diffusion of the products of communal human labor and the transition into the public domain as a movement from communal to universal human labor. As universal labor, science and technology are viewed as cumulative processes, which may then have some autonomy from the immediate economic base (Brown, 1987, 115) (the distinction of universal from communal labor, and its relevance to information systems, is more fully developed in chapter 7). A distinction between objectification and reification would also be relevant here: objectification would refer to the process of the transformation of knowledge into "organs of social practice, the real life process" (Marx, 1973a, 706); reification to allowing the thing like nature of technology to disguise the universal and communal labor embodied in it. Where information science has received technology as objectively given or as an autonomous development, if has fallen into the false consciousness of reification. The crucial points to be taken from the passage quoted from the *Grundrisse* are, then, that technology is a human construction, not a natural development, made historically and cumulatively, by human labor on nature, and that the materiality of technology is not denied but seen as the "the power of knowledge objectified."

An example may help understand these themes and appreciate the insights the perspective can yield. Consider, for instance, the contrast between the replication of the work of British novelists in the late-nineteenth-century United States, without copyright being accorded to the authors, and the distribution and reproduction of the Starr report. For the nineteenth-century works, copies were physically transported from Britain to American and then, in the case of the "cheap books" of the 1880s, reproduced by being reset by nonunionized labor, without proofreading (although the trans-Atlantic cable [1866] preceded the recognition of international copyright [from 1891], it does not seem to have been used for the transmission of novels, presumably because of the time and cost of signal production and transmission) (see chapter

3). The Starr report, in contrast, was first distributed electronically, with some reports of delays in signal transmission, and reproduced at the point of reception, for reading. Replication of the report as a published printed book, available for purchase, rapidly followed. There are familiar contrasts in the speed of dissemination and the effects this has on the significance of space and place (a concept of communication distance can also be found in Marx (Haye, 1980, 136, 151, 156). Beniger, for instance, regards speed as the most significant parameter of the control revolution (Beniger, 1986, 175). Precise numerical comparisons of speeds of transmission and replication may not yield great insights, but there may be a greater contrast in the pace of transmission, with physical transport replaced by signal transmission, than in the time required for reproduction, with automatic processes displacing human labor in typesetting. Far less noticed, but emerging forcibly from the perspective here, is the reduction in the quantity and skill of human labor required at the point of replication. A degree of historically accumulated universal labor and of communal labor was embodied in the late-nineteenth-century printing technology; greater physical and, particularly, intellectual labor, was embodied in late-twentieth-century communications and information technology; accordingly, less skill and understanding, and a lesser amount of labor, was required at the point of replication. The historical reduction of living labor required also exemplifies the fundamental dynamic of capitalism, the substitution of dead for living labor, although with regard to signal transmission and data transformation rather than the transformation of natural resources (see also chapter 7).

The distinction between objectification and reification can also be understood in relation to these examples. The "cheap books" (now rare) of the 1880s reveal their process of production by misprints and poor typography; analogously, delays in signal transmission indicated the humanly constructed nature of the Internet. For Marx

> it is by their imperfections that the means of production in any process bring to our attention their character of being the products of past labour. . . . In a successful product, the role played by past labour in mediating its useful properties has been extinguished. (Marx, 1976, 283)

A strong analogy can be made with the reconstruction in analytic bibliography of the diachronic filiations and the synchronic circumstances of production of a work from the transmission and commission of errors. Similar techniques have been used to detect citation of references from secondary sources. In these instances, the imperfections in the final products reveal their processes of production, bring the human labor involved in their making to attention. Reification would be more likely to occur when the finished appearance of the product disguises the labor embodied in it.

The view of technology as a human construction developed in the *Grundrisse* underlies the proposal for a history of technology given in *Capital*:

> A critical history of technology would show how little any of the inventions of the eighteenth century are the work of a single individual. As yet such a book does not exist. Darwin has directed attention to the history of natural technology, i.e. the formation of the organs of plants and animals, which serve as the instruments of production for sustaining their life. Does not the history of the productive organs of man in society, of organs that are the material basis of every particular organization of society, deserve equal attention? And would not such a history be easier to compile, since, as Vico says, human history differs from natural history in that we have made the former, but not the latter? Technology reveals the active relation of man to nature, the direct process of the production of his life, and thereby it lays bare the process of the production of the social relations of his life, and of the mental conceptions that flow from those relations. Even a history of religion that is written in abstraction from this material basis is uncritical. (Marx, 1976, 493-494)

The proposal (given and discussed more briefly in chapter 1) has been regarded as a prolegomenon to a history of technology which had yet to be written (N. Rosenberg, 1982, 34). Marx's concern is with forms of technology concerned with the human transformation of the material environment, but the extension of this perspective to information technologies, as a component of an information view of history, has been proposed (see chapter 1). Such a history remains even less written, but this chapter is itself intended as a contribution.

Some aspects of the passage again deserve comment. The view that mental conceptions flow from social relations can be regarded as an alternative formulation of the theme that being determines consciousness. The mediating role given to technology as the "basis of every particular organization of society" need not be regarded as technologically determinist, if the technology itself is regarded as a human construction, produced and adopted under specific historical circumstances. A significant critique of an emphasis on technique determining work relations further clarifies this position: for Marx, the "purely technical aspect is seen only as moment of the overall socioeconomic process" (Lukács, 1973, 55n); and the possibility of "*reciprocal interaction* by no means suppresses the real historical and methodological primacy of the economy over technique" (Lukács, 1973, 56). The reference to technologies as not the work of single individuals recalls the stress on the social intellect in the *Grundrisse* and anticipates the later categories of universal and communal human labor.

The reference to Darwin and natural technology does indicate the possibility of an evolutionary view of technology as a cumulative construction (N. Rosenberg, 1982, 6), but also exposes a crucial contrast. The "organs of plants and animals" are natural developments, whereas technology is a human construction, with domesticated animals as an example of human work upon nature. Humanly created technology is also revealed as equally important as "natural technology." The view of work, of productive labor on nature, as a condition of fallen human existence is reminiscent of *Genesis* and does place Marx in the Judeo-Christian tradition. The formula that men make their own history, here attributed to Vico, is central to Marx's thought. A subsequent notion in studies of technology, of path-dependency, could be regarded as exemplifying the qualification on this position, "but not of their own free will; not under circumstances they themselves have chosen but under the given and inherited circumstances with which they are directly confronted" (Marx, 1973b, 146). Vico might be more familiar from his view that the axioms as well as the subsequent propositions of mathematics are to be regarded as human constructions, not received as objects of contemplation (Vico 1988, 50-51; Warner, 1994), and does reinforce the possibility of discovering extensive analogies between critiques of technology and of mathematics or logic as objectively given.

The crucial points to be taken from this passage are the possibility of the historical study of technology as a cumulative human construction and the significance of those technologies to the production of social relations. For Marx, writing in the 1860s, it was only in large-scale industry that man had made objectified labor "perform gratuitous service on a large scale" (Marx, 1976, 510). From an information science perspective, information technologies can be regarded as comparably significant to industrial technologies to "every particular organization of society" (see chapter 1). Information technologies, developing extensively since the date of *Capital*, can then similarly be historically studied as cumulative human constructions.

On the basis offered by Marx, partly focusing on the crucial passages considered from the *Grundrisse* and from *Capital*, a modern understanding of technology has been constructed, particularly by Rosenberg (Mowery and N. Rosenberg, 1998; N. Rosenberg, 1976; 1982; 1994). Citation data simultaneously testifies to the influence of his work and to its relative lack of importation into information science. The diversity and complexity of technology is taken as axiomatic (N. Rosenberg, 1976, 2). Yet a degree of unity is also perceived:

> the most useful common denominator underlying its [technical progress's] multitude of forms is that it constitutes certain kinds of knowledge that make it possible to produce (1) a greater volume of output or (2) a qualitatively superior output from a given amount of resources. (N. Rosenberg, 1982, 3)

In an alternative formulation, technology is regarded as form of knowledge concerned with the transformation of natural resources into useful goods and services. The obdurate materiality of the machine is not denied but regarded as essential to its social function (Mackenzie, 1996, 9). In terms of the distinctions established, objectification, the transformation into of knowledge into part of the part of the real life process, is admitted, but reification, denying the human labor embodied in technology, is avoided. The difficulty of modeling technical change is conceded and it is recognized that only a rudimentary understanding of society's capacity for generating progress has been developed (N. Rosenberg, 1982, 29). In particular, the possibility of a qualitatively superior output, and not just its quantitative development, is significant but has not been sufficiently recognized by economics (N. Rosenberg, 1982, 3-4).

Information technology can be assimilated to this model. Drawing on the distinction derived from the discussion of the computer as a machine, it can be regarded as a form of knowledge concerned with the transformation of information inputs into information outputs, or, with potentially greater terminological clarity, with the transformation of signals from one form or medium into another. The understanding proposed deserves isolation and repetition:

> *A form of knowledge concerned with the transformation of signals from one form or medium into another.*

Again, at the first level of analysis, no distinction is made between the use of technologies in human communication and in machine control. Where the concern is with the complex technical antecedents to modern information technologies (Ohlman, 1996, 699), it may be helpful to treat the field in this unified, and undiscriminating, way; where the focus is specifically on human communication or on control, it would be helpful to introduce the further distinction (a distinction by function). The concept of "technology" has, then, been reinvigorated and discourse about information technologies productively linked to, but still differentiated from, discourse about other technologies.

A specific connotation is intended by *signals*, related to classic distinctions made in information theory, information science, and in semiotics. In *The Mathematical Theory of Communication*, the meaning of symbols was not relevant to considerations of the economic and efficient transmission of messages. A deliberately restricted sense of *information*, excluding meaning, was used. At the same time, optimism was expressed that the theory developed would be relevant to the understanding of human communication at the semantic level (Shannon and Weaver, 1949), and, this, together with the ordinary discourse connotations of information, has been a source for subsequent confusion. Bar-Hillel, in a well-known critique, reiterated and emphasized the distinction present in *The Mathematical Theory of Communication*, characterizing it as theory of signals, not information (Bar-Hillel, 1964). More recently, in information science, information as thing has been differentiated from information as process and information as knowledge (Buckland, 1991). Signals would carry the connotation of information as thing. An analogous distinction has also been made between dissemination, or message transmission, and diffusion, the growth of understanding, and, again, signals would correspond to the level of dissemination (Warner, 1997). In the rigorous, and potentially clarifying, terminology of Saussurean semiotics, the concern is with the signifier or expression (the term *signal* has itself been used for this aspect of the sign, in an English translation of Saussure), not with the signified or content, nor with the sign, the union of signifier and signified (Warner, 1994). Advantages in terminological clarity could be derived from the use of *signals* in preference to *information* and this move will be followed here.

Some attention should also be given to the understanding of knowledge, drawing partly on sources more familiar to information science and opening up the possibility of a reciprocal contribution to studies of technology. A distinction should be made, methodologically at least, between forms of knowledge open to symbolic, including verbal articulation (and a greater degree of exactness may be demanded by written rather than oral forms of verbal expression [Warner, 2001a]) and forms of knowledge resistant to reduction to symbolic form.

Even with forms of knowledge open to symbolic articulation, it would be wrong to identify the knowledge with its representation in a fixed text. Knowledge exists in a state of perpetual movement. To deny this is to exemplify it. There may be forms of knowledge transmission, for instance, didactic teaching (Collins, 1998), and forms of knowledge representation, such as the finished nature of a published book, which give it the appearance of relative fixity. In some discussions of the philosophy of mathematics, the interpretative assent of the relevant community is required to transform a written text into accepted knowledge. Analogously, in semiotics human interpretation is required to create signs from signifiers (Warner, 1994). Wiener distinguished between the texts published by scientists and their continual creation and re-creation of knowledge, memorably observing, "There is no Maginot Line of the brain" (Wiener, 1954, 122). An analogy could be made with the living labor needed to quicken the dead labor embodied in machinery (Marx, 1976, 527). A specific example of this analogy would be between a dead language embodied in a script which has not yet been deciphered and tools whose function is broadly recognized but for which the human knowledge of their specific use has not survived (and, historically, this been asserted of a cooper's tools). From this perspective, the knowledge embodied in technology is not located in the technology or its makers and users but must be continually recreated in the interaction between them. Knowledge, like the technologies in which specific forms of knowledge are embodied, can appear as a relation between things or as relation between men and things but is "*a social relation between men*" (Marx, 1976, 54).

Forms of knowledge resistant to symbolic articulation have been significant to the construction and use of technologies (N. Rosenberg, 1976, 78). At one level, certain forms of technology, such as nineteenth century United States agriculture, have been resistant to book learning, although this could be connected more directly with the relative cognitive authority attributed to local speakers and to books (P. Wilson, 1983) and with the locally variable conditions for agriculture (N. Rosenberg, 1976, 226). At a further level, the knowledge embodied in the development and use of technology may not lend itself to symbolic or theoretical articulation. The "theoretical conception [of how to execute a particular process] must be perfected by accumulated experience on a large scale" (Marx, 1976, 502). The resistance of such knowledge to symbolic articulation may explain the significance of the migration of personnel in technology transfer (N. Rosenberg, 1976, 154-155), although patterns of emigration have also been significant to the development of scientific, symbolically articulated, knowledge. With the late-nineteenth-century convergence of science and technology (Mowery and N. Rosenberg, 1998, 1-13), symbolically articulatable knowledge may have become more significant to advanced technology, and this would clearly be true of sophisticated forms of information technology, but the strong possibility of continuity with knowledge resistant to symbolic articulation must be allowed. Where knowledge is not reducible to symbolic form, which is then open to separation from its producer, it may retain its human origins more transparently.

An example of a technology in use, of a steamboat on the Mississippi, may help to understand and substantiate these themes:

> "Did you ever know of a boat following a bend upstream at this stage of the river?"
>
> "No, sir, — and I was n't trying to follow it. I was getting away from a bluff reef."
>
> "No, it was n't a bluff reef; there is n't one within three miles of where you were."
>
> "But I saw it. It was as bluff as that one yonder."
>
> "Just about. Run it over."
>
> "Do you give it as an order?"
>
> "Yes. Run over it."
>
> "If I don't, I wish I may die."
>
> "All right. I am taking the responsibility."
>
> I was just as anxious to kill the boat, now, as I had been to save her before. I impressed my orders upon my memory, to be used at the in-

> quest, and made a straight break for the reef. As it disappeared under our bows I held my breath; but we slid over it like oil."
>
> "Now don't you see the difference? It was n't anything but a *wind* reef. The wind does that."
>
> "So I see. But it is exactly like a bluff reef. How am I ever going to tell them apart?"
>
> "I can't tell you. It is an instinct. By and by you will just naturally know one from the other, but you will never be able to explain why or how you *know* them apart."
>
> It turned out to be true. The face of the water, in time, became a wonderful book – a book that was a dead language to the uneducated passenger, but which told its mind to be without reserve, delivering its most cherished secrets as clearly as if uttered them with a voice. (Twain, 1984, 93-94)

It may be worth recalling that Wiener's deliberate reinvention of the term *cybernetics* was a testimony to the pilot's concern with control mechanisms (Warner, 2001c; Wiener, 1954).

The non-verbal signals read from the river surface are made into signs by human interpretation. Those signs can be spoken about but cannot be given direct verbal equivalents — "you will never be able to explain why or how you *know* them apart." For passengers, the surface of the water remains a "dead language," whose significant, rather than physical, aspect, may not be even be known to them, and who, even given this awareness, might not be able to isolate individual signs. An analogous situation existed historically with cuneiform, which was received as natural marks rather than a human semiotic construction. Without the semiotic interpretation, the boat remains inert machinery, loses both use- and exchange-value when deprived of contact with living labor (Marx, 1981, 527). In terms of the previously established distinctions with regard to information technology, the concern here is with control mechanisms in a transport technology.

The knowledge involved in the piloting of the boat is transmitted by direct apprenticeship, whose completion requires an immersion in detailed experience. The design and construction of the boat itself embodies the cumulative experience of its constructors. In use, the boundary between the machine and its environment is a matter of convention, a theme present both in studies of technology and of automata: for Marx, anticipating the discussion of the location of knowledge, for large scale machinery, "the skill resides not in the worker but in the machine and in the scientific combination of both as a whole in the factory" (Marx, 1976, 529n); analogously, in automata studies, the question of where a particular machine ends and its environment begins can only be settled by convention or definition (Minsky, 1967, 19). Despite the hard materiality of technology, it resembles a language, in which the point of view creates the object (Saussure, 1983). The knowledge in use of the technology resides in the collective of pilot and apprentice, boat, and river surface. In the intervals between human interaction, the "system of machinery . . . constitutes in itself a vast automaton . . . driven by a self-acting prime mover" (Marx, 1976, 502), and here there is a specific analogy with one sense of nondeterminism in automata theory, where a series of automatic transformations continues until an ambiguous configuration is reached and the process halts until a human choice is made (Warner, 1994).

Invention, innovation, and diffusion

Within the modern understanding of technology as a human construction, a series of systematic distinctions, derived from Schumpeter, is made with regard to the dissemination and adoption of technologies. At the greatest level of granularity, conceptualization, invention, innovation, and diffusion are differentiated, understood as follows (N. Rosenberg, 1976, 192-93).

- Conceptualization — The idea for a technology
- Invention — Establishment of technical feasibility
- Innovation — The commercially feasible product
- Diffusion — The subsequent adoption and spread of the innovation.

In less finely differentiated, and possibly more standard, accounts conceptualization is not distinguished as a separate phase (Freeman, 1987). A debate exists as to the sharpness or rigidity of the distinctions, and, contrary to a rigid interpretation of the Schumpeterian framework, it is argued that minor movements in a technology can have cumulative significance: innovation is only the beginning of the diffusion process and an innovation may be substantially changed in character in diffusion (Nelson, 1969; N. Rosenberg, 1976, 66-81; Stolpher, 1969). It is also acknowledged that the relation between these stages may change historically, for instance, with the transformation of invention from a private into a corporate activity. It is tempting to apply a phrase derived from considerations of the relation between expression and idea in U.S. copyright, a continuum of similarity, but to still to regard distinctions along the continuum as indicating analytically valuable, and substantively real, differentiations.

The need for these distinctions in information science can be sensed from their absence in studies of information technology, with conceptual confusion resulting, and from their presence in inchoate form, without reference to the clarifying framework (Ohlman, 1996; Warner, 1994, 40). A comparative reading would suggest firmer adoption of distinctions in media studies (Howells, 1999). Their adoption within information science should clarify its own treatment of information technologies and also make available a framework within which the historical perspective of information, and, in this instance, library, science can be used to explore the sociotechnical dynamic associated with information technologies.

The significance and value of the distinctions may be better understood when they are compared with analogous distinctions made with regard to scholarly communication, which are well established within information science. For instance, conceptualization could be regarded as analogous to a dialogue with oneself, or, at a further stage, informal conversations with colleagues; invention compared to reduction to writing; innovation to publication, which itself need only be regarded as a binary event for certain purposes (Kling and McKim, 1999, 897); and diffusion to adoption of a text or idea by scholarly communities. Not distinguishing innovation from diffusion for information technologies would be tantamount to compounding publication and communication. Further, for both publication and adoption, there are known indicators (bibliographic records for publication and citation data for adoption). For these, an important distinction is made between the indicator and the phenomenon, which might escape detection by the indicator or reveal itself in other ways. Similar methodological reservations will be placed on the indicators to be proposed here, for assessing innovation and diffusion of information technologies.

In summary, the series of distinction from conceptualization to diffusion are to be regarded as analytically valuable, if not essential, distinctions, for information as well as productive technologies. Historians of industrialization have been preoccupied with invention, possibly as it may be easier methodologically to isolate, in the first instance, and have neglected diffusion. Yet the social and economic consequences of technological changes are a function of their rate of diffusion and not the date of their first use. From the perspective of world history, the critical social process requiring examination is diffusion (N. Rosenberg, 1976, 173). As part of the study of the diffusion, we should seek to understand how the superiority of a technology came into being rather than ascribing it to inherent qualities of the technology. A similar focus of attention on invention can be discerned in studies of information technologies (Ohlman, 1996) and a comparable shift would be equally desirable.

Summary

Technology is to be regarded as a radical human construction, adopted under specific historical circumstances. It is viewed as a social relation between men which may appear as a relation between men and things or between things and things, but this false appearance should be dissolved. Information technology was differentiated from productive technology, by its concern with the transformation of signals, not natural resources. A further distinction between of use of information technologies in human communication and in machine control was proposed. The concept of "knowledge", either as existing in human interaction or as embodied in technology, was not reified but neither was the materiality of the machine denied. Crucial distinctions, relating to the invention and adoption of technologies, were introduced. Further projects, part of an information view of history (see chapter 1), can now be foreshadowed.

Information View of History

From an information view of history, a number of crucial questions can be identified.

- First, given that diffusion, not invention, is taken to be of primary significance, what indicators for diffusion can be supplied?
- Secondly, what was the critical period for innovation and diffusion of modern information technologies (preliminary evidence indicates the late-nineteenth-century United States)?
- And, thirdly, why did innovation and diffusion occur at that time and in that place?

Other, comparably, although not necessarily equally, significant, questions can be asked and have begun to be addressed (Warner, 2001a) but these are sufficient opening topics, which can be briefly outlined here.

Registering of innovation and diffusion in copyright

The history of copyright represents a rich and largely, although not entirely (Warner, 1990; 1993a), unexploited resource for tracing the development and impact of information technologies. A focus on copyright will give a bias toward human to human, and public not private, communication, rather than control mechanisms (although some media impacting on copyright, such as musical or piano rolls, could be regarded both as control mechanisms and as part of human communication). This distinction is at least acknowledged, in contrast to an exclusive focus on control mechanisms (Beniger, 1986), and an emphasis on communication and transport as a whole may be more convincing. Patent would reveal only invention, and, although the chronological gap between invention and diffusion testifies to the significance of the distinction (consider the typewriter, for instance), the focus here is to be on diffusion and, to a lesser extent, on innovation.

Copyright registration and legal deposit provide, in differing ways, indicators of the proliferation of nonbook forms. Copyright registration in the United States was essential to claims for copyright, until the *Berne Convention Implementation Act 1988* allowed to copyright to subsist, but not necessarily to be fully asserted, without prior formalities (see chapter 3). Both legislation and, with greater numerical detail, copyright registrations then provide an explicit record of the assimilation of nonbook forms to copyright protection. Legal deposit in the political regions governed by the United Kingdom (the pedantry of the phrase is only justified by its accuracy as deposit was extended throughout the British Empire) has not been fully required for copyright since the late nineteenth century. A less numerically precise indicator of the nonbook forms is, however, provided by the gap between claims for copyright as intellectual property and works received under legal deposit (Warner, 1990). The level of impact for nonbook forms given by these indicators can be placed on the continuum from innovation to diffusion. For both jurisdictions, imperfect and historically variable, collection and recording practices will have to be considered (Solberg, 1939; Warner, 1990).

Some control mechanisms and codes used in human to human communication (for instance, telegraphic codes) have impinged on copyright (Warner, 1993a) and this can yield a further indicator of the development of information technologies. A nontechnical approach would be to regard the costs of litigation and of legislation as deterring action unless the artifact in question has acquired a certain level of social significance. A complementary approach, informed by the distinctions developed here, would be to regard copyright litigation as evidence of innovation, for there must be at least two competing parties disputing ownership of intellectual property (and not simply an invention without commercial significance). Even denial of protection by the judiciary is indicative of innovation. Copyright legislation would then be taken as indicating diffusion, with the social costs of producing knowledge in exact, written form (N. Rosenberg, 1976; Warner, 2001a) taken as discouraging legislation in response to relatively isolated innovations. Empirically, this distinction of innovation from diffusion can be supported by the pattern of technologies impinging on the judiciary, traditionally regarded as oriented towards precedent, and the subsequent correction of anomalies arising by the legislature (Warner, 1993a), concerned with current and future public good.

The history of copyright can, then, provide highly specific indicators of information technology innovation and diffusion. If attention is primarily focused on the United States and the United Kingdom the geopolitical limitations of the study must be acknowledged, although a geopolitical, as well as chronological, parameter is simultaneously provided. The indicator adopted needs to be distinguished carefully from the phenomenon, which, it is recognized, may elude the indicator or emerge in other ways. For fuller understanding, evidence derived from copyright would have to be viewed in relation to other indicators and placed in the context of developments in control, communication, and transport as a whole.

Critical period for modern information technologies

Evidence from the history of copyright which could illuminate information technology innovation and diffusion has been partially accumulated and made public by Warner (1990; 1993a), but for contrasting, although related, purposes. The chronology presented here can be read diachronically or synchronically (see Figure 2.1). The approach will be to read each category diachronically but to comment on the synchronic patterns rendered visible.

The formal history of legal deposit for the United Kingdom can be read from United Kingdom legislation. For the *Copyright Act 1842*, single, inherited definition of a book encompassed a work for deposit and for intellectual property; for the *Copyright Act 1911*, a book for legal deposit was differentiated from literary and other works for intellectual property. Although not directly revealed by the formal history of legislation, deposit began to be rigorously and extensively enforced from the 1850s and 1860s (Warner, 1990). Closely concurrent, and possibly slightly earlier, signs of the diffusion of nonbook forms can be found in United States legislation for media to be covered by copyright registration. The *Copyright Act 1870* conferred the registration of copyrights and the deposit of works on the Library of Congress, establishing registration procedures appropriate to the material form of the work. The divergence of legal deposit and copyright as intellectual property for the United Kingdom is confirmed by the *Copyright Act 1911*; legislation for copyright registrations for the United States indicate the diffusion of nonbook materials from the mid-1860s.

Copyright cases in the United Kingdom are indicative of innovations in shorthand and telegraphic codes in the mid-1880s and of musical (or piano) rolls from the late 1890s. Despite their extensive diffusion in the United States, telegraphic codes do not emerge as subjects of judicial dispute until 1921. Musical or piano rolls feature in a well-known, if not notorious, case of 1908, *White-Smith v. Apollo*. In the case of musical or piano rolls, anomalies arising from the judicial denial of protection were deliberately corrected by legislation in 1909

(United States) and 1911 (United Kingdom) (a view that *White-Smith v. Apollo* was not fully overruled by the *Copyright Act 1909* did, however, dominate [Warner, 1993a]). The *Copyright Act 1870* expanded the range of forms protected in the United States and from the 1870s onwards a liberal, or inclusive, interpretation was given to the constitutional clause, the "writings of an author." International conventions, indicative of increasing international communication begin from the 1880s. The relative autonomy of the United States is revealed in its refusal to accede to those conventions, although the possibility of recognizing international copyright was opened up from 1891 (see chapter 3). Evidence from litigation (corresponding to innovation) and, more fully and convincingly, from legislation (indicative of diffusion) strongly the suggest the 1870s as a crucial period for the development of modern information technologies, again with developments occurring slightly, but significantly, earlier in the United States.

Other developments, including those in the more narrowly construed information and library sphere, support the significance of the mid- to late nineteenth century. Panizzi's historical moment occurs when transport and communication had made the wide enforcement of legal deposit possible, although public communication was shortly to be driven beyond the forms captured by deposit. The Library of Congress was broadly concurrently transformed from a government library into an institution of national significance. H. G. Wells's speculation on the world brain (Rayward, 1999) follows the empirical possibility of global, or near global, communication through signal transmission. These developments could be regarded as further instances of being, partly mediated through technology, determining consciousness. Information technology developments (derived from standard accounts of invention, which acknowledge that dates for inventions must be approximations) cluster from the mid–nineteenth century, with a particularly intense phase in the 1870s. The presentation here, if read synchronically from left to right, does at least give ontological priority to forms of the social over the technical.

The 1870s and 1880s have, then, been compellingly identified as the crucial period for innovation and diffusion for modern information technologies, with the United States, and, to some extent, links between the United States and Europe, as highly significant loci. This is in sharp contrast with assumptions of the recency of modern information technology, which has influenced discussions of the information society concept (Webster, 1995a). However, it is congruent with other accounts: with Beniger's chronological, and geopolitical, location of the control revolution and account of the development of modern communication technologies (Beniger, 1986, 7-20); with the understanding of globalization as a late-nineteenth-century movement in communication studies (Mattelart, 1996); and with Wells's early understanding of global communication (Wells, 1902). The geopolitical, as distinguished from the chronological, locus identified seems to have been less anticipated.

Why at that time and in those places?

Radical changes in information and communication technologies, as distinct from cumulative developments in existing innovations, are rare in world history. Such technologies have more often constituted a relatively stable backdrop to more dynamic events (Collins, 1979, 63). The question of why this nexus of developments should have occurred at that time and in those places must, then, be addressed.

The late nineteenth century United States is familiarly regarded as the age of invention. Mark Twain's personal involvement in unsuccessful innovative enterprises and fictional representations, in *The Gilded Age* and *A Connecticut Yankee in King Arthur's Court*, are well known. For one aspect of the innovation of the period, the American system of manufactures, or the production of standardized goods from specialized machines with interchangeable parts, an explanation has been given for its emergence first in the United States. On the demand side, high aggregate demand for certain classes of commodity, which could be connected with the expanding population of the period, enabled production processes whose profitability required long runs. The limited variety in composition of the demand encouraged the use of highly specialized machinery. On the supply side, there was a rich abundance of natural resources, not reduced by extensive consumption by previous technological developments. Processes that were resource wasteful, but economically rational, could then be adopted (N. Rosenberg, 1994, 109-120). Readers of Fenimore Cooper will recall reiterated references to "the white man and his wasty ways" and the conditions of the period have been suggested as the roots of American profligacy with natural resources. In summary, labor scarcity and natural abundance pushed rapidly towards rich inventive possibilities (N. Rosenberg, 1994, 109-20).

Further conditions for technological dynamism and creativity can be distinguished. The essential dynamic of capitalism is innovatory:

> Modern industry never views or treats the existing form of a production process as the definitive one. Its technical basis is therefore revolutionary, whereas all earlier modes of production were essentially conservative. (Marx, 1976, 617)

Capitalism, in this sense, emerged in particularly pure form in the late-nineteenth-century United States:

> Nowhere does the fluidity of capital, the versatility of labour and the indifference of the worker to the content of his work appear more vividly than in the United States of North America. In Europe, even in England, capitalist production is still affected and distorted by hangovers from feudalism. (Marx, 1976, 1014n)

A contrast is made with the merely stable labor power of the slave. The account of labor mobility and the fluidity of capitalism is consonant with the fictional representations of the period. Crucial dimensions would be expanding territory and population and the absence of a constraining inheritance.

These conditions would enable invention and innovation in information and communication technologies, but not, given the high rate of failure in innovation, account for their diffusion and adoption. The pivotal position of the market, and of communication in the market (commerce and communication share a common etymology), must be recognized (Haye, 1980). A further, more historically specific, demand for signal transmission over space would have been created by frontier expansion and the developing links with Europe. The rapid diffusion of the telephone and the telegraph can, in different ways (Sola Pool, 1977), can be understood in this context. The closing of the frontier is dated to 1880, shortly after the diffusion of a nexus of communication technologies and concurrent with their continuing development. A thematic link is thereby created to the, still powerful, frontier hypothesis, which takes the existence of an area of free land (assimilating, in its original form, conquest to expansion) and the continual recession of the frontier as crucial to American economic and cultural development (Grossman, 1994a; 1994b; Turner, 1996; see also chapter 3).

A preliminary explanation has, then, been given for the diffusion of information and communication technologies in the late nineteenth century United States and between the United States and northwest Europe. Even if other geopolitical regions were to be identified as sites for innovation and adoption (dates for diffusion in Europe, implied by the proliferation of international treaties from the 1880s, indicate a slight but, but still significant, lag), the explanation for the United States would remain valid. The converse or absence of the crucial factors identified might be relevant to the suggested lag, for instance, the legacy of feudalism in Britain (Porty, 1977), and, for France, with its large internal distances, the envisioning of communication as proceeding from the state to the individual (Attali and Stourdze, 1977; Mattelart, 1996), in contrast to American democracy and populism.

Conclusion

A largely novel view of information technology as a radical human construction, carefully differentiated from productive technology, has been developed, drawing on themes derived from Marx, and mediated by economics, and combining these with understandings established in automata studies and information science. An account was given of critical distinctions, from invention to diffusion, developed in economics, which could then be applied to information technologies. Data from the history of copyright, and, for the United Kingdom, from legal deposit, little known outside information and library science, was used compellingly to suggest the late-nineteenth-century United States as a crucial time an place for modern information technology innovation and diffusion. An explanation for the adoption of information technologies was given in terms of the technological dynamism and geopolitical expansion and communication of the period.

The understanding of information technology developed needs refinement, and the evidence and explanation given for its diffusion requires expansion and development, but the possibility of a valuable intra- and extradisciplinary contribution has been opened up.

Figure 2.1. Chronology of registering of information technology developments in copyright.

Date	United Kingdom Case	United Kingdom Legislation	United States Case	United States Legislation
1826				
1839				
1842	*Copyright Act 1842.* A work in which copyright could inhere was to be "construed to mean and include every volume, part or division of a volume, pamphlet, sheet of letterpress, sheet of music, map, chart, or plan separately published."			
1844				
1846				
1854				
1860				
1861				
1865			*Copyright Amendment 1865* Extended copyright to photographs and their negatives.	
1866				

Chrononology ***continued.***

International Convention	Other Developments	Information Technology Development	Date
		Photography	1826
		Microphoto-graphy	1839
			1842
		Baltimore - Washington telegraph	1844
	Smithsonian Institution established		1846
		Sounder telegraph	1854
	Panizzi's historical moment	Typewriter (reliable). Pony Express.	1860
		Trans-continental telegraph	1861
	International Telegraph Union		1865
		Trans-Atlantic cable	1866

Chrononology *continued.*

Date	United Kingdom Case	United Kingdom Legislation	United States Case	United States Legislation
1870			*Copyright Act 1870.* Extended protection to "painting[s], drawing[s], chromo[s], statue[s], statuary, and ... models or designs intended to be perfected as works of the fine arts."	
1876				
1878				
1880				
1884	*Pitman v. Hines.* Concerned with copyright in shorthand. *Ager v. Peninsula.* Concerned with telegraphic codes.			
1886	*Ager v. Collingridge.* Concerned with telegraphic codes.			
1891			*Copyright Amendment 1891.* Nonresidents and noncitizens could be recognized as copyright holders.	
1895				
1896				
1897				
1899	*Boosey v. White.* Concerned with musical (piano) rolls.			
1901				

Chrononology *continued.*

International convention	Other developments	Information technology development	Date
	Library of Congress transformed into an institution of national significance.		1870
		Telephone	1876
		Phonograph	1878
	Closing of United States frontier.	Hollerith punched card machine	1880
			1884
Berne Convention 1886			1886
			1891
		Cinematography	1895
		Wireless telegraphy	1896
		Pianola (player piano)	1897
			1899
		Radio	1901

Chrononology *continued.*

Date	United Kingdom Case	United Kingdom Legislation	United States Case	United States Legislation
1908			*White-Smith v. Apollo* Concerned with musical (piano) rolls	
1909			*Copyright Act 1909.* A musical roll could constitute a copy of a score. The musical roll itself, and comparable contrivances, were not to be regarded as writings.	
1911	*Copyright Act 1911.* The category of a "literary work" was introduced to United Kingdom copyright legislation and replaced that of a book in 1842 Act, as an artifact in which copyright could subsist. A literary work was to be interpreted as including "maps, charts, plans, tables, and compilations." The definition of a book for deposit was largely unaltered from the 1842 Act but confined to a separate section.			
1917	*Anderson v. Lieber.* Concerned with telegraphic codes.			
1921			*Reiss v. National Quotation Bureau.* Concerned with telegraphic codes.	

Chrononology *continued.*

International Convention	Other Developments	Information Technology Development	Date
Berlin Convention 1908			1908
			1909
			1911
			1917
			1921

Chapter 3

Information Society or Cash Nexus? A Study of the United States as a Copyright Haven

In the four quarters of the globe, who reads an American book?

— Sydney Smith, 1820

Sydney Smith writing in the *Edinburgh Review* in 1820 could continue to ask rhetorically: "or goes to an American play? or looks at an American picture or statue?" (quoted in A. Bell, 1980, 210). The remark, and the strong reaction to it (A. Bell, 1980, 210), was to resonate sufficiently through nineteenth-century American consciousness to include persistent quotation and allusion in copyright judgments. By 1996, it could be suggested that the McDonald's sign was better known worldwide than the cross. More broadly, the extent of U.S. economic influence has ensured the dissemination of the symbols associated with its consumer products.

Between the two extremes indicated by Sydney Smith and revealed by contemporary advertising lies a neglected aspect of American history: the status of the U.S. as a copyright haven from 1790 to 1891 (1). From the Copyright Act 1790 that limited copyright to United States citizens and residents to the Chace Act 1891 that enabled reciprocal copyright agreements to be established with other nations, foreign authors' intellectual property rights could not be asserted within the United States. The copyright haven existed, then, from the maturation of the modern concept of copyright as an author's right in the late eighteenth century until the late nineteenth century, the longest known copyright haven of significance. The works of foreign authors, particularly those of English-language novelists, were subject to extensive printing without compensation to the author. The concern here is not primarily with the details of the events, disputes, and campaigns associated with the absence of copyright for foreign authors and with the movement for international copyright, although the richness and fascination of the primary material deserves exploration and re-presentation, but with the broader social, political, and economic conditions that encouraged the transition marked by the Chace Act. The contrast between Sydney Smith and contemporary advertising, between the localization and the export of communication, will form at least a partial basis for explanation.

The consideration of the context of the Chace Act is relevant to two current concerns. First, there are interesting, if uncomfortable, analogies between the nineteenth-century United States as a copyright haven and late-twentieth-century China as an exploiter of U.S.-produced videos, CDs, and computer software without observing copyright. Secondly, the suggestion that economic developments were critical to the 1891 transition in information policies is relevant to the idea of information as an autonomous variable found in discussions of the information society (2). Each of these contexts can be indicated in turn.

There are a number of similarities and contrast between copyright in the nineteenth-century United States and late-twentieth-century China. A principal commonality is the use of material copyrighted in other nations without the permission of, or compensation paid to, holders of copyrights. Some dissimilarities lie in: the nature of the copyrighted material used; the legislative sanction given to the unrestricted use of foreign works in the United States in the period to 1891 as contrasted with the contravention of agreements in late-twentieth-century China; and differing understandings of copyright, particularly with regard to the conflict of freedom of expression and dissemination of information as contrasted with personal property rights. A factor that should be emphasized, and that forms one rationale for this chapter, is the disturbing lack of historical consciousness in current discussions of intellectual property relations between the United States and China. The general lack of references to the United States as a copyright haven in these discussions (Oppenheim, 1993; *Economist*, 1996), combined with a rather moralistic tone, does give the impression of a collective forgetting or repression.

In the concept of a postindustrial or information society, associated for instance with Bell (D. Bell, 1980), there has been a stress on the autonomy of information and on the role of theoretical knowledge as a director of social change:

> The axial principal of the postindustrial society, however, is the centrality of theoretical knowledge and its new role, when codified, as the director of social change. (D. Bell, 1980, 509)

The idea of a transition to an information society, symbolized by the computer, has tended to be conceived as a radical disjunction, a "turning point[s] in modern history" (D. Bell, 1980, 509-44). Other studies have also emphasized radical change. For instance, an important source for the changing status of knowledge in the postmodern age is Jean-François Lyotard's *The Postmodern Condition: a Report on Knowledge* (Lyotard, 1979). For Lyotard, too, these changes are connected with the development of computing and telecommunications:

> It is reasonable to suppose that the proliferation of information-processing machines is having, and will continue to have, as much an effect on the circulation of learning as did advancements in human circulation (transportation systems) and later, in the circulation of sounds and visual images (the media). (Lyotard, 1979, 4)

In such assertions, there are traces of technological determinism in the stress on the autonomous significance of the computer. In other discussions, the computer itself has been characterized as a "radical novelty" (Dijkstra, 1989), implicitly viewed in isolation from other, pre-existing and continuing, information technologies (Warner, 1994; 2001b).

In this context the intention is to explore the contrast between a stress on the autonomy of information and an emphasis on the economic basis of social activity. The latter perspective received its classical expression in Marx:

> The totality of these relations of production constitutes the economic structure of society, the real foundation, on which arises a legal and political superstructure and to which correspond definite forms of

> social consciousness. The mode of production of material life conditions the general process of social, political and intellectual life. It is not the consciousness of men that determines their existence, but their social existence that determines their consciousness. (Marx, 1975, 425)

A stress on the significance of the economic base need not be reduced to a crude economic determinism, although it has sometimes been interpreted as if it were, for instance by Bertrand Russell in *The Practice and Theory of Bolshevism* (Russell, 1920). From a perspective that stresses the determining power of the economic base, information would tend to be regarded as a dependent rather than an autonomous or primary variable, which could still complexly interact with the economic base.

Despite the significance of the issue there seems to have been limited attempts at exploring or resolving the contrast between the idea of information as a primary or autonomous variable and an emphasis on the influence of the economic base, particularly within the literature of information science. The issue can be addressed by theoretically informed empirical studies of the autonomy of information. One study of a carefully delimited domain, of information sources on the information producing activities of an information organization, concluded that only a limited autonomy could be ascribed to information, in that context (Warner, 1988). Empirical studies of information in broader social contexts can be complicated by the difficulty of isolating the information components of complex social activities and of establishing relations of causality between information and economic or social developments. This chapter looks at one context in which information developments can be isolated, for analytical purposes, and studied in relation to economic and social factors: the development of a highly significant, if partly forgotten, aspect of U.S. copyright.

The United States as a Copyright Haven

Studies of the United States as a copyright haven do exist (Bishop 1959; Clark, 1960) but they have certain limitations that can plausibly be connected with the circumstances of their production. The date of appearance of these studies precedes the development of extensive copyright piracy of computer software and other nonbook media by developing countries and the public diffusion of the concept of an information society. A published study (Clark, 1960) emerges from a classic bibliographic perspective, not informed by later calls for a sociology of texts (McKenzie, 1986), and largely adheres to the implicit understandings of a genre of narrative history that concentrates on the influence of the principal individuals and formalized groups on a historical process. A rather moralistic tone is assumed, with an immediate equation of the legal use of material with copyright piracy, and the stress on judgment can impede sympathetic explanation. The topic of international copyright tends to be viewed largely in isolation from its broader context and transitions in copyright legislation can be given a rather improbable causal role. In particular, the 1891 recognition of foreign authors' copyrights is credited with giving a significant impetus to the development of American literature. From the bibliographic perspective that implicitly informs the work, documentary communication tends to be equated with literature as novels, drama and poetry, with little attention given to emerging significance of formal international communication in commerce, science and technology in the second half of the nineteenth century. Despite the limitations it shares with the genres from it emerges, the study is highly valuable for its historical detail and bibliographic references (Clark, 1960). The relative lack of recorded citations to studies of the United States as a copyright haven gives the sense that the collective forgetting partially extends to more narrowly scholarly contexts.

The status of the United States as a copyright haven has received only limited attention from other, potentially interested, scholarly communities. Legal commentaries on copyright tend to concentrate on precedents that are thought not have been overruled and on currently applicable legislation and to give only cursory attention to its historical development (Abrams, 1991; McCarthy, 1991; Nimmer, 1990). Where the issue has been addressed from a legal perspective (Patterson, 1968, 198-200) it has been found difficult to explain the limitation of copyright benefits to citizens and residents. The disciplines that supply the chosen context for explanation, economic and social history, give very limited attention to copyright in pre-1891 America (M. K. Cayton, Gorn, and Williams, 1993; John, 1993; Porter, 1980). A literature search did not discover any previous study that contextualizes the American refusal of foreign copyright in the nineteenth century or that relates it to current copyright concerns or to the information society concept.

The more formal history of the denial of copyright to foreign authors, as revealed in legislation and significant cases, can be reviewed. The Constitution granted Congress the power: "to promote the Progress of Science and useful Arts, by securing for limited Times to Authors and Inventors the exclusive Right to their respective Writings and Discoveries" (Constitution, 1789). Although there is limited evidence from which to reconstruct constitutional intentions with regard to copyright, it may have been influenced in this by the contemporary idea of the natural rights of the author as a creative individual (Ringer, 1985, 26). The first Copyright Act of 1790 explicitly and carefully denied protection to non-U.S. citizens and limited the benefits of copyright to citizens and residents of the United States (Copyright Act, 1790). These provisions were to persist through the various amendments and general revisions of copyright legislation until 1891 (Copyright Act, 1802; 1831; 1865; 1870; 1882) although they were not subjects of the legislative debates connected with those amendments and general revisions (Clark, 1960, 90-1 and *passim*). However, in view of the vehemence of discussion of international copyright in other contexts, they must be regarded as deliberately reinstated not as an unexamined legacy.

The clarity of the statutory provisions on citizenship and residence may explain why they were infrequently tested in the courts (Copyright Decisions, 1909). The few interventions recorded dispute the interpretation of residence rather than the binary, and readily documented, dichotomy of citizen/alien. The effect of significant judgments was to strengthen or reinforce residence requirements. Most significantly, in *Boucicault v. Wood* (1867), it was held that an author's residence was to be determined by intention, as evidenced by acts, not simply the duration of stay. A more technical clarification followed the *Copyright Act 1870*, which had extended protection to a range of new media. The judgment held that the addition of lithographs and the like to the list of potentially copyrightable items did not indicate an intention to change the understanding of proprietor as other than resident or citizen (*Yuengling Jr. v. Schile*, 1882). The relative lack of case law may have partially disguised the significance of the citizenship and residence provisions of the period to 1891 to commentaries on copyright.

The *Chace Act 1891* enabled the United States to begin concluding bilateral agreements, formal copyright treaties and various proclamations, with other countries. Foreign citizens were to be subject to the benefits of the Act only when their nation granted U.S. citizens copyright on substantially the same basis as their own citizens, or,

> when such foreign state of nation is a party to an international agreement which provides for reciprocity in the granting of copyright, by the terms of which agreement the United States of America may, at its pleasure, become a party to such agreement. The existence of either of the conditions aforesaid shall be determined by the President of the United States by proclamation made from time to time as the purposes may require. (*Copyright Act*, 1891)

For instance, assurances from Belgium, France, Great Britain and the British Possessions, and Switzerland, that their law permitted United States citizens the benefit of copyright on substantially the same basis as to the citizens of those countries rapidly enabled the extension of copyright benefits to the citizens of those countries (Proclamation, 1891). Extension to Germany and Italy was to follow in 1892 (Proclamation, 1892a, 1892b). The provision introduced in the 1891 Act known as the "manufacturing clause," which, in summary, prescribed that English language works were to manufactured in the United States, was retained.

There are substantial contrasts between the pre-1891 United States and contemporary Europe in copyright practices. Intellectual property rights of aliens and nonresidents were explicitly protected, beginning from the early nineteenth century onward, first by legislation by individual nations, then by reciprocal treaty, and, finally, by the Berne Convention. Copyright havens did exist but in more restricted senses, and either in retaliation against the United States, or, more briefly, in connection with new media. As early as 1838, Great Britain had indicated its readiness to enter into a reciprocal treaty with the United States, but, in the absence of action from the United States (Clark,

1960, 80), continued not to observe American authors' copyrights, unless they were asserted by a combination of first publication and presence at the time of publication. As the *Encyclopaedia Britannica* article on copyright wryly noted in 1911: "the injury to British authors was greater only in proportion as the English works were more numerous." (*Encyclopaedia Britannica*, 1911). Slightly more analytically, is has been asserted that Great Britain was the greater pirate before 1850 and the United States after 1850 (Clark, 1960, 50). A short-lived copyright haven in Great Britain in piano rolls and other media for the reproduction of music developed from at least the period of the judgment in *Boosey v. White* that held that such rolls were to be regarded as "parts of a mechanical contrivance for producing musical notes" and were not appropriate subjects for copyright (Boosey, 1931, 145-8; *Boosey v. White*, 1899, 574-75; Skone-James, 1948). The judgment was deliberately corrected by the *Copyright Act 1911* (Copyright Act, 1911). The general reciprocal observance of copyright within Europe does highlight by contrast the anomalous position of the United States among industrializing and informationally significant nations.

The scale and rapidity of the publishing activities in the United States made possible by the absence of copyright in foreign authors' works should be recognized, although it is difficult to generate numerical data that is both accurate and meaningful. In 1842, it was claimed that the employment of more than 160,000 people depended on the book trade (including the publication of domestically originated material) (Clark, 1960, 69). Dickens's *American Notes*, in which he scrupulously avoided mention of the copyright disputes that had marked his visit in 1842 (Dickens, 1982; Forster, 1928, 214), was published in 1843, with a pirated edition selling 50,000 copies in three days (Clark 1960, 78-9). Pirating by periodicals was developed and *Harper's Monthly*, founded in 1850 and almost entirely dependent on appropriated material, had a circulation of 200,000 by 1860. In terms of speed of reproduction, it is indicative that newspapers issued novels as extras and that, in one instance, Harper's issued the three volume *Peveril of the Peak* in 21 hours (Clark, 1960, 36 and 78-9). Price differentials between Great Britain and the United States were marked: for instance, Dickens's *A Christmas Carol* was issued in 1843 at $0.06 in the United States and the equivalent to $2.50 in England (Clark, 1960, 40). Two considerations arise from the scale and rapidity of these activities. First, if legislation against reprinting without observing foreign intellectual property rights had been enacted in mid-nineteenth-century American would it have been enforceable in the context of the strength of the popular sentiment for the practice? Secondly, the speed of reproduction may be comparable with modern technologies, particularly when considered in relation to conditions of transport and communication. Greater human labor at the point of reproduction is required.

The character of the publishing activities enabled by the absence of copyright in foreign works shows some change over time (M. K. Cayton, 1993). Publishing of foreign material had little apparent commercial significance before the 1830s, but the contemporary vogue for Walter Scott was accompanied by the increased exploitation of English language novels. Periodicals dependent on material reproduced without observing copyright began to develop from the 1850s. The period 1870-1891 saw the growth of inexpensive reprint series, known as "cheap books," which were not produced by regular publishers with other publishing activities (with the exception of Harper's Franklin Square Library), were set by female, nonunion and poorly paid, labor and were not proofread. Books could become ancillaries to other commodities, given away with soap cakes, or, as whole sets with a 50-cent bottle of medicine (Clark, 1960, 30-31). An increasingly deliberate commercialization of publishing activity can therefore be observed throughout the period, intensifying in the 1870s and 1880s (M. K. Cayton, 1993).

Opposition to the absence of copyright in foreign works came from a number of parties, British and American authors, and, finally, under changed conditions of domestic market instability, from United States printers, publishers and typographic unions (Clark, 1960). These groups, particularly the authors, reiterated two themes in their arguments: natural justice and the natural rights of the individual; and the brake placed upon the development of American literature by the ready availability to publishers and readers of much less costly British material. Dickens's first speech on copyright during his 1842 visit captures both themes and would seem likely to have been informed by reading and discussion:

> I hope the time is not far distant when they [authors], in America, will receive of right some substantial profit and return in England from their labours; and when we, in England, shall receive some substantial profit and return for ours. . . . There must be an international arrangement in this great respect. . . . It becomes the character of a great country; first, because it is justice; secondly, because without it you can never have, and keep, a literature of your own. (quoted in Chesterton, 1925, 142)

Proponents for international copyright seem to have unquestioningly endorsed the right of the individual to derive economic benefit from the products of his or her intellectual labor.

The arguments offered in defense of the continued denial of intellectual property rights to foreign authors tended to concentrate on refuting the practical points made by their opponents and not to address the issue of abstract property rights. Where they do raise issues of principle, they assert the right to protect domestic labor or the value of unrestricted circulation of literature (Clark, 1960, 52-77). A representative petition stresses the latter issue:

> All the riches of English literature are ours. English authorship comes to us as free as the vital air, untaxed, unhindered, even by the necessity of translation; and the question is, Shall we tax it, and thus impose a barrier to the circulation of intellectual and moral light? Shall we build up a dam, to obstruct the flow of the rivers of knowledge? (Sherman & Johnson of Philadelphia presented to the Senate and the House, June 13 1842. Quoted in Clark, 1960, 77)

Although there is some resemblance here to the conflict of free speech and public good (the progress of science and useful arts) with property rights in intellectual productions that later discussions of copyright have found (Nimmer, 1986; P. Wilson, 1990; see also chapter 7), there is no evidence of explicit questioning of the principle of copyright.

The principal arguments offered for and against the recognition of foreign copyright remained relatively stable over time, from the late 1830s to the early 1880s. In the 1880s, additional arguments and political pressures were brought by other groups, publishers, printers, typographic unions and librarians, in favor of copyright. If we are to account for the changed outcome of established arguments in terms of legislation, and for the addition of other themes and pressures, we must attend not just to the arguments themselves but to the changed conditions of their production and reception.

The predominant characteristic of the period from the 1830s to the 1880s would seem to be the development of the United States from little more than a collection of populated places east of the Mississippi River, loosely bound together by coastal and inland water transportation, into a unified market and a rapidly industrializing nation (Martin, 1980). The period is marked by political isolationism and a refusal of European influence in American affairs, a set of attitudes and policies that came to be labeled as part of the Monroe doctrine. The myth and reality of entrepreneurial capitalism were felt to coincide, even from some radical perspectives. For instance, it has been suggested that the United States held a similar place in the public imagination to the Soviet Union in the early 1930s (Warner, 1983).

A crucial factor differentiating the American experience from that of Northwest Europe, where many immigrants had originated and that also contained nations significant to the development of copyright, is the western expansion and settlement. In contrast to Northwest Europe, settlement and economic growth took place concurrently (Easterlin, 1980). The importance of the frontier to American consciousness has been stressed (Grossman, 1994a; Turner, 1996) and its significance to American economic development and to copyright should also be recognized. We do not need to accept the equation of settlement with conquest, nor the marginalization of the native populations, in the development of the frontier thesis (Grossman, 1994a; Limerick, 1994; White, 1994), in order to value its empirical content as a description of U.S. expansion. The concurrence of settlement and economic development has been considered to explain the distinctive features of American population growth, particularly its extent and duration (Easterlin, 1980), and it would also seem to have a wider implication (for the connection with the development of information technologies, see chapter 2). Critical factors in common with Northwest Europe in terms of copyright development are the linguistic and cultural links, particularly, although not exclusively, with the English language.

In summary, the thesis presented here will be that the concurrence of spatial expansion and economic development created a continuously growing internal market, with little dependence on the import or export of material goods, and, at that stage of development, limited needs and resources for the export of information products. Transitions, first informally and then formally, begin to occur from the 1870s, with a diminishing rate of growth of the internal market, the closing of the internal frontier, and the diffusion of more sophisticated and internationally linked information practices within the United States. The closing of the frontier, effectively in the late 1870s (Grossman, 1994a; Turner, 1996) shortly precedes the confluence of interests and persuasions that resulted in the 1891 Act. Specific topics, and their relevance to copyright practices, can be examined within this broad framework.

The period 1865 to 1900 was one of rapid economic growth. In 1865, the United States was a culturally and economically backward nation of less than 35 million people. The development of the railroad was critical in bringing all sections of the country into the national economy, or, more accurately, enabling the creation of a national economy. One characteristic of a national economy is the regional differentiation of productive functions (Martin, 1980) and the growth of the printing and publishing industries can be regarded as one aspect of this. The period also saw a decline in the relative importance of agriculture, although only slowly until the mid-1890s, from 74 percent of the people living on farms in 1870 to c.33 percent of Americans engaged in agriculture in 1910. Conditions would then seem to favor a release of labor from agricultural to cultural, scientific and technological activities, and, according, both an increased demand for and then output of associated information products.

The population of the United States grew throughout the period from 1790 to 1900, although with varying rates of growth. The very high rates of growth from 1790 to 1860, averaging 3 percent per year, began to decline after 1860, accompanied by a diminished rate of distribution among regions but with an increased rural-urban movement. Immigration was also a continuous feature of the period 1860-1900 (Easterlin 1980). From the perspective of the demand for reading matter and of copyright, two significant factors can be indicated: the high levels of literacy (Gilmore-Lehne, 1993), which, together with population growth, created an expanding market; and the linguistic links with Northwest Europe, historically inherited and sustained by immigration. Population figures usually given are c.13 million in 1830, 35 million in 1865, and 76 million in 1900 (R. L. Cayton, 1993; Easterlin, 1980).

The issue of foreign trade, not just in information goods, would also seem to be crucial to an understanding of the historical context of the Chace Act. Until the 1840s, the United States was heavily dependent on its export sector to sustain development. Thereafter, the expanding internal market became more significant (with the exception of enforced foreign trade during the Civil War). Exports had fallen to less than 6 percent of GNP by 1860 and a policy of tariff protection of domestic labor was in place. From the 1870s, export activity begins to rise and from the mid-1870s, the value of exports was to exceed the value of imports in almost every year until the 1950s. The nature of the exports in the period 1880-1900 also reflected the increased sophistication of the U.S. economy. It included processed agricultural and manufactured goods (including information technology products such as typewriters). Public concern over dependence upon Europe as a destination for imports grew in the 1890s. Tariffs continued to rise but were slightly ameliorated by reciprocal agreements with other nations. From 1900 onward, with the de jure accession to the gold standard and the attempt, together with Great Britain, to keep China open to trade with all industrialized nations, the sharp differentiations between the foreign trade policies and practices of the United States and other industrialized nations seem to have been diminished (Rothstein, 1980). With regard to copyright, it can be seen: that the limited dependence on import-export activity would tend to negate the effect of sanctions that might have otherwise been imposed by nations whose intellectual property rights were being exploited; and that the transition to honoring foreign authors' copyrights is broadly concurrent with increased export activity.

The period 1800-1890 also witnessed striking developments in communications. The predominant form of communication among colonial and immediately postindependence American businessmen had been direct oral communication and the handwritten letter, with the letter particularly used for exchanging information about distant markets. The development of transport technology in the form of the railroad had a significant and dual effect: first, as a carrier of mail it enabled the more rapid interchange of correspondence (McClelland, 1980); secondly, together with improvements in printing technology and paper manufacturing, encouraged the development of newspapers and magazines that communicated business information (Madison, 1980). A partial analogy can be detected with the development of scientific or scholarly communication, where, characteristically, oral and semiformal communication among interested parties may develop into published journals (Watson and others, 1973). The adoption of information technologies for the transmission of messages over space from the 1840s onward, first the telegraph and then the telephone, further assisted the development of a national market (Madison, 1980). The earlier innovation, the telegraph, is more significant in this period, and, in a similar way to trade, internal development preceded foreign connections. By 1865, there were 200,000 miles of telegraph line but a successful cable operation between England and America was not in place until 1866 (Madison, 1980). With regard to copyright, these developments in transport and other communications are reflected in the transition from registration by state, with provisions made for national deposit (Copyright Act, 1790; Copyright Act, 1831), to both registration and deposit on a national basis (Copyright Act, 1865; Copyright Act, 1867; Copyright Act, 1870).

The development of science and technology could be expected to stimulate a demand for the free exchange of documentary information. Technology can be regarded as a special form of knowledge dealing with the transformation of the material environment into useful goods and services (N. Rosenberg, 1980) (on this model information technology could be regarded as a form of knowledge concerned with the transformation of signals from one form or medium to another) (see chapter 2). Some forms of technology, including mid-to-late-nineteenth-century American agriculture and branches of heavy industry, have tended to be resistant to innovation and book learning (N. Rosenberg, 1980). Technological inventions can be developed by individuals without scientific education and practical understanding of technological processes can, and has, preceded scientific explanation of their operation. Yet the late nineteenth century in the United States emerges as a critical period for the adoption of interconnected technological innovations (including forms of information technology) (Beniger, 1986; Segal, 1993). Twentieth-century technological innovation was to become more dependent on scientific knowledge, in, for example, the fields of chemistry, electronics, and biology (N. Rosenberg, 1980).

Science in the United States shows increased signs of development and modern forms of institutionalization from the mid-nineteenth century: for instance, Massachusetts Institute of Technology was founded in 1861; in the 1870s and 1880s the scientific community began to grow and become more professional in character, including the development of domestic graduate education (Thelin, 1993), professional associations and scholarly journals; and, in the early twentieth century, American corporations began to fund research activities intended to develop technology in conjunction with science (Reich, 1980). Scientific communication in developed nations had become embodied in the scientific journal, which assumed its subsequent dominant role from the 1860s onward (Bradford, 1948), and, in contrast to literature, which may be deliberately regional or national in character, science tends to have an ideology of internationalism. A position of parity with the major European powers is considered to have been reached by American science by the early twentieth century (Numbers, 1993).

These developments in science and technology would seem likely to encourage, first, a demand for full access to relevant literature produced in other regions (and importation for use was to be permitted under the manufacturing clause), and, secondly, a concern that the circulation of American journals and the contribution of American scientists to foreign journals should not be affected by any sanctions that might be imposed in connection with inequalities in copyright. Some empirical support for this speculation can be found in the support of university presidents, publishers, and the American Library Association for the 1891 Bill (Clark, 1960, 163-81). The focus of discussions of the movement for international copyright has tended to be on the circulation of and property in literature, construed principally as fiction, drama, essays and poetry. Yet it is also possible to discern the increasing significance of other forms of documentary communication, connected with the development of science and technology.

There were, then, in the period from 1830 to 1890 significant developments in the economy, population, foreign trade, technology, and science of the United States. From the 1870s onward, the internal frontier was closing and the United States was adopting patterns of education, documentary communication and research that were likely to encourage reciprocal communication with Europe through formal mechanisms. A desire that internal and external communication should be relatively stable and well regulated would also seem likely to emerge.

Some more familiar, and more specific, indicators of level of information development can also be considered. The period 1865-1870 also marks the growth of the Library of Congress from an institution primarily supporting the information needs of government into to an entity with national library functions (Goodrum, 1986). The institution of deposit for the use of the Library of Congress is broadly coincident with, although slightly subsequent to, the more rigorous enforcement of legal deposit throughout Great Britain and its possessions (Ollé, 1986). In this context, both developments can be seen as dependent upon improved transport and communications, particularly a national postal service. Copyright registrations and deposits for the period to 1891 are known to be incomplete (Solberg, 1939) and registration would not include publications for which copyright was not claimed. However, the expansion of the term "writings" to include nonverbal forms of writing and nondocumentary material, including new media such as photography, from the 1870s onward has been recognized (Holland, 1978; Warner, 1993a) and does indicate the increased diffusion of information technologies. From these indicators, then, the 1870s emerges as a critical period for the adoption of more sophisticated information practices within the United States.

In the context of these economic, social, political, and, more narrowly, information, developments what explanations can be given for the transition in copyright practices marked by the 1891 Act? Following the closing of the internal frontier, and the economic development of settled lands, the United States was beginning to export material and information goods and to develop patterns of education, research and documentary communication comparable to major European powers. It had, then, to some extent to conform with the copyright practices of this group. The power of the United States is revealed in the manufacturing clause, which itself is a testimony to the influence of printing interests. The stimulus offered by the Berne Convention to the implementation of international copyright, and the threat in the Convention (Berne Convention, 1886) to deny copyright to United States productions for which the stratagem of first publication in a member country was used, must be seen in this broader context. The level of information development reached by the United States from the

1870s was comparable with Northwest Europe, and, particularly, Great Britain, its English language counterpart, and implies a need for reciprocal communication and partly comparable information practices. The disruption to the internal market, its increasingly anarchic character, in the 1870s and 1880s, and the effect this had to persuade publishers and unions to support international copyright (Clark, 1960), can also be seen in this broader context. For instance, the saturation of the market following the closing of the internal frontier can be suggested as a cause for the development of "cheap books." The concern of publishers with works from U.S. authors, and their circulation in Europe, can also be seen as a partial explanation for their support for international copyright.

Conclusion

Significant aspects of the history of copyright in the United States can, then, be read to suggest that economic and political developments slightly precede and, plausibly, influence information developments. The possibility of economic disadvantage rather than advantage in continuing to ignore foreign authors' claims to copyright is followed by the conclusion of bilateral agreements. The late nineteenth century emerges as a critical period for the increased adoption of a range of information technologies and for the development of a convergence in copyright practices between politically separate regions.

A proposition with regard to copyright can be advanced on the basis of this empirical study: that copyright protection is only extended, or enforced when extended by legislation, to imported intellectual products when the costs associated with nonextension or nonenforcement approach the benefits obtained from the absence of copyright in those products (3). These benefits could include, and for the nineteenth-century United States did include, a low price for access to and dissemination of valued information, effectively avoiding payment for the labor invested in its development. Costs of nonextension or enforcement of copyright need not be construed in narrowly economic terms, although this is a significant aspect of possible costs. They could include limited participation in extranational political communities, as well as reciprocal exploitation of the products of domestic intellectual labor, and an unstable internal market for information products.

A number of similarities and contrasts can be detected between the nineteenth-century United States and late twentieth-century China and the more significant can be mentioned here. A principal commonality is the non- or limited recognition of rights in foreign intellectual property. The linguistic link with Northwest Europe and the internal expansion accounted for the continuance and duration of the United States as copyright haven. There is not a comparable linguistic link between the United States and contemporary China, but the exploited forms (such as computer software, recorded music and film) are not necessarily primarily composed of oral or written languages, although they may contain extensive elements of them. For instance, computer programs can be regarded as a form of writing not closely linked to a spoken language and never intended as a communicative substitute for speech (Warner, 1994), although software products may contain verbal components.

Contrasts can also be seen in the legality of actions, with China introducing although not fully enforcing copyright legislation on the Western model (*Economist*, 1996), whereas United States statutes excluded foreign and nonresident authors from protection. Differences also exist in relevant historical contexts and in understandings of copyright. In China before the 1949 revolution, some copyright legislation existed but the act of copying was regarded as indicative of respect in Chinese culture. From a classic Marxist perspective, which would have influenced post-1949 China, the "function of bourgeois copyright is to establish a monopoly on the sale of the work, which is treated as a commodity." More value is also attached to dissemination than to monetary reward to the author (Gringal'ts, 1973).

The constraints imposed on the autonomy of legislators by the difficulty of containing copyright issues within national boundaries have been widely recognized (U.S. Congress, Office of Technology Assessment, 1986; Nimmer, 1990). Yet, on the evidence here, the origins of this development have to be dated to at least the mid-nineteenth century, for European nations, and can be connected with the influence of transport as well as information technologies. The possibilities for nations, in different ways and for different durations, to escape the compulsion of international conformity, should also be acknowledged.

The contrast between the idea of information as a primary and autonomous variable and a stress on the determining power of the economic base has still to be addressed. A reading of significant aspects of the history of copyright in the United States indicated that economic developments slightly precede and strongly influence information developments. On this analysis, it would be misleading to regard information as a primary or autonomous variable, and, without reverting to a crude economic determinism, more productive to acknowledge the strong influence of the economic base.

A central claim associated with the information society concept has, then, to be rejected. Yet, rather than discarding a concept as rich and suggestive as that of the information society, it can be productively modified. For instance, in sociology the theme of the informatization of life has been developed. Informatization is understood as the increased significance attached to information activities and their increased pervasiveness in contemporary societies. Economic influences on information developments are acknowledged and explored. Informational developments are understood in terms of historical antecedents and continuities. The idea of an abrupt disjunction in the transition to an information society is also questioned (Webster, 1995a, 1-5, 217-18). While acknowledging that the scope for willed or imposed change may be circumscribed, information technologies can be used to good or ill. The fuller the understanding of information developments, and the deeper our historical consciousness, the more deliberately, and, perhaps, productively, our future can be influenced.

Notes

1. The term *copyright haven* is the standard historical term used to refer to the legal exclusion of foreign and nonresident authors from copyright protection in this period. In contrast to the phrase, copyright piracy, it emphasizes the legally sanctioned nature of this exclusion. It also avoids prejudgments, which might obscure historical insight, as to the morality or legitimacy of the practice.

2. The phrase in the title of the paper, "cash nexus", is an allusion to Carlyle's lament for the replacement of feudal order by unregulated mercantilism:

> to what shifts is poor society reduced, struggling to give still some account of herself, in epochs when Cash Payment has become the sole nexus of man to man! . . . Cash Payment the sole nexus; and there are so many things which cash will not pay! Cash is a great miracle; yet it has not all power in Heaven, nor even on Earth. (Carlyle, 1971, 195-199)

The phrase is echoed in *The Communist Manifesto* (Marx and Engels, 1998, p.37).

3. This proposition would seem to be broadly congruent with the more formalized analysis of costs and benefits offered by Braunstein (1987), although that analysis does not allow for the case of complete absence of recognition of rights in imported products of intellectual labor.

Chapter 4

As Sharp as a Pen: Direct Semantic Ratification in Oral, Written, and Electronic Communication

> Nay, sure, he's not in hell: he's in Arthur's bosom, if ever man went to Arthur's bosom. 'A made a finer end, and went away an it had been any christom child; 'a parted ev'n just between twelve and one, ev'n at the turning o' th' tide; for after I saw him fumble with the sheets, and play with flowers, and smile upon his fingers' end, I knew there was but one way; for his nose was as sharp as a pen, and 'a babbl'd of green fields.
>
> — *Henry V. Act II. Scene III.* [Report of the death of Falstaff]

> From: Jo Moore
> To: Alun Evans; Mortimer, Robin
> Date: 11/09/01 14:55:12
> Subject: Media Handling
>
> Alun
> It's now a very good day to get out anything we want to bury.
> Councillors expenses?
> Jo
>
> CC: Corry, Dan
>
> — Tuesday September 11, 2001, Whitehall memo. *Guardian Unlimited*, 2001.

The phrase "as sharp as pen" has been read primarily literally, as description of Falstaff, and has been difficult to reconcile with his corpulence. Falstaff's activities — "fumble with the sheets, and play with flowers, and smile upon his fingers' end" — are regarded as traditional signs of impending death, as is the skeleton appearing through the flesh (Shakespeare, 1995, 82). The phrase can also be read metaphorically, with the harshness of writing contrasted with the human voice speaking the passage and with the dialogue reported. The source of the metaphor is first the physical sharpness of the pen, for scratching or inscribing, in accord with the technical origins or early development of writing (Harris, 1986, 26), and, secondarily but possibly more strongly, the possibility of cruelty in distant and remote communication. There is also a familiar association between writing and death, in the context of a report of the death of Falstaff. The e-mail message sent on September 11, 2001, exemplifies, rather than alludes to, the potential absence of compassion in remote communication. It also painfully illustrates difficulties with e-mail as a medium.

My concern here is with understanding difficulties with electronic communication, particularly e-mail. Other, publicly reported, instances of inappropriate communication could be adduced. Readers may also wish to reflect on their communicative conduct, on messages they have sent or received, and on the regret or resentment they have experienced. The legislative framework will not be addressed, except allusively, but we will be concerned with the evidential status and value of different forms of communication. E-mail, and other forms of electronic communication, will be understood historically, in terms of a combination of the dynamics of oral and paper written communication.

Acknowledging an influence from the medium to the content of the message need not be regarded as technologically determinist, if the technology itself is regarded as a human construction, produced, maintained, and renewed by human labor (see chapter 2). In the adaptation of a classic Marxist perspective on productive technology, the possibility of "reciprocal interaction by no means suppresses the real historical and methodological primacy of the economy over technique" (Lukács, 1973, 56). From this perspective, proposing technical constraints, for instance, the delaying and accumulation of e-mail messages for sending, as a sufficient solution to difficulties experienced emerges as not necessarily technologically determinist but influenced, possibly unconsciously, by technological determinism. Like repression, simply imposing technical constraints might encourage issues repressed to emerge in other forms. A more productive approach lies in a deeper understanding of communicative behavior, which can then inform conduct. The medium is regarded as encouraging, but not compelling, certain forms of communication.

Direct Semantic Ratification

I wish to introduce a dimension known as direct semantic ratification and to explore its significance in relation to oral, paper written, and electronic, predominantly verbal, communication (1). The term is slightly technical, not fully present in ordinary discourse, but does comprehend a range of relevant and valuable components. More familiarly, I will also be concerned with the evidential status and value of different forms of verbal communication, as this is relevant to the possibility of litigation, disciplinary action, or exposure, following inappropriate communications.

Direct semantic ratification has classically been understood, in an early, although still significant, study of orality and literacy, as both exemplified and developed by direct oral communication:

> The intrinsic nature of oral communication has a considerable effect upon both the content and the transmission of the cultural repertoire. In the first place, it makes for a directness of relationship between symbol and referent. There can be no reference to "dictionary definitions," nor can words accumulate the successive layers of historically validated meanings which they acquire in a literate culture. Instead, the meaning of each word is ratified in a succession of concrete situations, accompanied by vocal inflections and physical gestures, all of which combine to particularize both its specific denotation and its accepted connotative usages. This process of direct semantic ratification, of course, operates cumulatively; and as a result the totality of symbol-referent relationships is more immediately experienced by the individual in an exclusively oral culture, and is thus more deeply socialized. . . . The language is developed in intimate association with the experience of the community, and it is learned by the individual in face-to-face contact with the other members. (Goody and Watt, 1968)

Face-to-face communication implies that other elements of communication, for instance, facial expression and intonation, may be significant. The concept of direct semantic ratification has been adopted, to some extent, by subsequent discussions of orality and literacy and partly transformed. For instance, Ong notes that the meaning of each word in oral discourse is controlled by "direct semantic ratification," *understood* as the opportunity for questioning the producer of a statement and for immediate knowledge of the context in which it was produced (Ong, 1982, 47).

An analogous concept has also been independently formulated. The idea of "autoglottic space" has been developed and regarded as crucial to understanding how written language restructures primarily oral thought, particularly the development of formal logic. *Autoglotttic* is understood as language without a human voice, exemplified by written language, "a form of unsponsored language which is not limited to particular categories of speech act or verbal practice" (Harris, 1989, 104). In this context, we are not concerned with the historical impact of unsponsored language on the possibilities of thought but with autoglottic as a dimension of current communicative significance. Independent discovery of an analogous, or, more strictly, complementary and opposing, concept to direct semantic ratification could be regarded as an instance of incomplete dialogue in the scholarly sphere, but also as a conformation of the significance of the concept. Autoglottic does introduce a further component not fully captured by direct semantic ratification and crucial to the idea of evidence. With autoglottic sentences, there is no immediate link of utterance to utterer and the connection may have to be reconstructed from nonverbal evidence. We will also be concerned, then, with the nature of the link between utterance and utterer and with the evidence needed to establish or confirm that link.

I wish here to introduce an additional, if already partly implicit, component of corporeal presence and to understand.

- Direct semantic ratification as the possibility of immediate dialogue between participants in a conversation, physically, culturally, and linguistically proximate to one another.
- Removal from direct semantic ratification as distant physically, in time and space with diminished corporeal presence, and as possibly involving cultural and linguistic diversity, with an emphasis on the diminishing of the dialogic character of the utterance.

Where the significance of direct semantic ratification has been recognized, it has been regarded as a highly consistent, although still not absolute, factor differentiating oral from written communication (Biber, 1988). Rather than seeking to establish differentiations between oral and written communication, it may be more productive to acknowledge the significance of the dimension but to regard it as distributed across oral, written, and electronic communication, in ways that are simultaneously simple and more complex, and that confirm its significance. The dimension may be more significant than the specific medium.

Oral communication

Different levels of direct semantic ratification and contrasting values as evidence can be distinguished for different forms of oral communication, from interactive oral communication, which can be contrasted with forms of oral communication in primary orality for which direct semantic ratification is deliberately denied, to recorded oral communication.

Interactive oral communication could be regarded as offering the greatest possibility of direct semantic ratification. We speak with our whole body and there are paralinguistic elements of expression, intonation, and body language, in addition to the verbal content of utterances (Harris, 1986). The significance attached to interactive oral communication, and to nonverbal elements of linguistic performance, persists in literature cultures in legal cross-examination, and, in British parliamentary practice, in question time for the Prime Minister. The aim in legal cross-examination may not be so much to elicit information as to entangle the person examined in contradictions or to expose discrepancies between their verbal utterances and their body language. The value attached to these forms of interactive oral communication represents an informal, but still powerful, grasping of the significance of direct semantic ratification.

The evidential value of interactive oral communication can be limited. Unrecorded, and not independently witnessed, utterances can be recalled as testimony but can also be denied or distorted.

Oral communication can be monologic rather than dialogic in nature, even in primary orality. Dialogue was forbidden at spoken oracles and verbal accounts and visual representations indicate limited or not visual contact between the ritual speaker and the enquirer (Aune, 1987). A further example from drama can exemplify these themes:

> Banquo. How far is't call'd to Forres? – What are these,
> So wither'd and so wild in their attire,
> That look not like th'inhabitants o'the'earth,
> And yet are on't. Live you? or are you aught
> That man may question? You seem to understand me,
> By each at once her choppy finger laying

Upon her skinny lips: you should be women,
And yet your beards forbid me to interpret
That you are so.
. . .
1 Witch. Banquo and Macbeth, all hail!
Macbeth. Stay, you imperfect speakers, tell me more.
. . .
Say from whence
You owe this strange intelligence? or why
Upon this blasted heath you stop our way
With such prophetic greeting? – Speak, I charge you
[*Witches vanish.*] (*Macbeth.* Act I, Scene III)

Dialogue is refused nonverbally by the witches, by the laying of finger upon lips. A consideration of spoken oracles enforces a recognition that: not all forms of communicating in primary orality are dialogic in nature; where oral communication is not dialogic it is regarded as incomplete and demanding interpretation, anticipating the exegetical forms of enquiry associated with the influence of written language. The significance of the dimension of direct semantic ratification is further confirmed.

Recorded or transcribed oral communication may acquire evidential value, although the interpretation of utterances can still be disputed. Knowledge of recording or transcription can inhibit the immediacy and liberty of participants in dialogue. It is also possible to conceive of instances where a written transcription has been agreed and is credited with greater cognitive authority than recording (this would be exemplified by records of parliamentary debates).

Written communication

Semantic ratification has been regarded as not occurring with written language. It would be more convincing and productive to suggest that that it is modified rather than absent, with channels for interaction reduced and a delayed dialogic character. In a sense, semantic ratification may be less direct than with interactive oral communication. In its original formulation, autoglottic was understood to be exemplified by written language, in that unlike oral communication, it did not have a sponsor. The concept of autoglottic space may also have to be modified, recognizing that certain forms of written communication do have sponsors: for instance, an article in a scholarly journal can be regarded as sponsored by the author or authors and by the journal itself, as a social construction, embodying refereeing and editorial procedures. The role of semantic ratification and autoglottic space in relation to written language can be further understood by considering on restricted domain of written communication, scholarly communication.

Scholarly communication is conducted dialogically. In informal conversations and conference presentations, there is a combination of monologue and dialogue. In the fully public, permanent, and written contributions, directed to addressees remote in time and space, semantic ratification is present but delayed. For instance, a citation or book review could be regarded as dialogic responses of varying depths. Within information science, this viewpoint would be familiar from the conversation model of scholarly communication. A dialogue in the public domain between a single author at different points in time can still be assimilated to this model (P. Wilson, 1983). From a perspective within linguistics, a book has been regarded as a "*verbal performance in print*" intended for "organized, *printed* reaction in the various forms devised by the particular sphere of verbal communication in question (book reviews, critical surveys, defining influence on subsequent works, and so on)." Even where a work is nominally oriented towards an abstract addressee, for instance, the common reader, that addressee is inevitably perceived through the social milieu of the author and their scholarly communities (Vološinov, 1986). A strongly analogous model of scholarly communication by oral and written interaction over space and time has been apparently independently developed in the sociology of philosophy (Collins, 1998). Semantic ratification is, then, delayed and less immediate, with channels reduced and some depersonalization, rather than blotted out, with this form of written communication.

Scholarly communication, like many other forms of writing, demands intellectual labor. Classically, it has been said that, what is written without effort is generally read without pleasure. The intellectual labor embodied in published writings formed the basis for the labor or "sweat of the brow" understanding of copyright (see also chapter 7). Intellectual labor is also applied in the various filtering and modifying processes that precede publication: editing, refereeing, copy-editing, and the like. One effect of the intellectual labor applied is to prevent, or at least restrict, rhetorically inappropriate contributions from reaching the public domain.

Some other written forms do not demand as much intellectual labor as scholarly publications (and for those forms in which only a limited degree of intellectual labor has been invested, copyright may not inhere). Yet the role of copyediting alerts us to the expectation of grammatical and orthographic correctness. In contract, in oral speech, even the speech of literate subjects, incompleteness is accepted and we may not hesitate over correct forms. Oral utterances can also be of contrasting degrees of formality.

The physical labor required for the production of written utterances can also be considered. Physical labor is intense with some historical, and still continuing forms of writing, such as monumental inscriptions, still strong (and individually variable) with handwriting, diminished with typewriting, and further reduced with word processing systems.

The evidential character of written communication can be considered, with some attention to the concept of autoglottic space. Written communications can notoriously be produced as evidence, although there may still be disputes over their interpretation once a relatively unambiguous copy has been agreed. In some circumstances, the evidential value of an utterance may depend on establishing a link from utterance to utterer. A written utterance can be divorced from its producer and become autoglottic. Nonverbal evidence may then be needed to transform it from an autonomous utterance into one known to produced at a specific time and place, by human agency, linked to a particular utterer or utterers. Conversely, direct oral utterance could generally be clearly linked to its producer (with ventriloquism regarded as diabolic) but was difficult to produce as evidence.

In summary, then, for written communication, semantic ratification exists but is delayed, with channels reduced, and is less direct, when contrasted with direct oral interaction. The intellectual and physical labor involved in the production of written utterances may enforce deliberation and filter out rhetorically inappropriate contributions. Writing has evidential value but may not be immediately linkable to a specific producer.

Electronic communication

Electronic communication, particularly e-mail, can be regarded as combining elements of oral and written communication. It has some of the fluidity of oral communication, without the constraining personal or corporeal presence of the addressee, with diminished direct semantic ratification. It also retains some of the permanency and evidential value of writing.

Direct semantic ratification is not fully present at the point of production of the utterance, without the personal and corporeal presence of the addressee. An addressee distant in space is presumed and addresser-addressee roles may be more clearly demarcated than for interactive oral communication. Iconic signs in e-mail messages could be regarded as an attempt to import an illusion of personal presence, to compensate for the impersonality of writing. Semantic ratification does occur, at an interval longer than for oral communication but characteristically shorter than for paper correspondence or published scholarly communication. Communications can also have a marked dialogic character, resembling responses in an oral conversation.

The intellectual and physical labor in production required for e-mail communication may be limited. Messages are often short personal or quasi-personal communications rather than intellectually demanding forms. Physical labor in production is less than for hand and typewriting and may be further diminished by the use of abbreviations. The labor in production is analogous to oral rather than formal written forms of communication. In contrast, the intellectual labor in interpretation is not radically altered compared to other forms of written communication and close scrutiny of messages received would be possible.

E-mail also has the evidential character of other forms of written communication in its permanency, in addition to its susceptibility to scrutiny. It may be more be more analogous to printed rather than hand or typewritten communication, in that it does not bear personally specific traces of its production. There is no direct equivalent to the substrate to assist in determining the circumstances of production of a message, or to ensure its deletion. Its evidential value could also be limited by its autoglottic character as a detached sequence of signals, which do not necessarily conclusively link the utterance to a specific utterer: if the apparent producer denies having produced an utterance, circumstantial evidence, such as its time and place of production, may have to be sought.

In summary, then, e-mail communication: lacks the constraining presence of the addressee at the point of production of the utterance; provides semantic ratification at an interval between the immediacy of interactive oral communication and the delay of paper correspondence, and, further, of published communication; requires limited intellectual and physical labor in production, with an acceptance of informality developed; but retains some of the permanency and evidential character of other forms of writing. The fluidity of speech can lead to indiscreet utterances. Delayed, but still rapid, dialogic interaction can induce "flaming" of responses, which, in direct oral communication, might have been constrained by the presence of the other. Unlike oral communication, utterances are permanent and can readily be recalled as evidence and subjected to scrutiny.

Conclusion

The dimension of semantic ratification, and the degree of directness, has emerged as crucially important. It is distributed across oral, writing, and electronic communication in ways that confirm its significance and is crucial to understanding the dynamics of electronic communication.

The legal context has not been directly addressed although the evidential value of electronic communication has been considered. Published accounts of disputes suggest that litigation or disciplinary action tends to occur after acceptable conduct has been continuously breached. A strategy for avoiding litigation would be to understand and, by understanding, to influence and possibly modify our communicative conduct. There may also be elements of social as well as individual learning. It is unusual for communication theory or models practically to inform our conduct at the level of pragmatics, or the human effects of communication, rather than at syntactics, the structuring of messages, or empirics, signal transmission.

The theme of excluded corporeality has also emerged as significant. It has been suggested, in a study of Internet pornography, that the body has been excluded from the study of electronic communication (Cronin and Davenport, 2001). In this context, it has been reintegrated as one aspect of direct semantic ratification. Excluded corporeality could be regarded as a Cartesian inheritance, where the mind is detached from the body: "the Cartesians situate the human spirit in the pineal gland, as if it were an observatory" (Vico, 1988, 88). When semiotic phenomena are separated from physical human presence, they become difficult to interpret.

A humanistic and historical perspective has informed the approach here. From this viewpoint, the introduction of written language to primary orality has been regarded as enabling the development of formal logic and a logico-empirical, rather than mythical, modes of thought: philosophers, who "may be regarded as the old men of the nations, founded the world of the sciences thereby making humanity complete" (Vico, 1976, 167). A more scientific and fully empirical, possibly experimental, perspective, informed by the distinctions developed here, would be possible.

Note

1. Following Mark Twain in *Fenimore Cooper's Literary Offenses*, *verbal* is understood as both spoken and written language and *oral* as spoken language only (Twain, 1994, 389).

Chapter 5

In the Catalogue Ye Go for Men: Evaluation Criteria for Information Retrieval Systems

Ay, in the catalogue ye go for men;
As hounds, and greyhounds, mongrels, spaniels, curs,
Shoughs, water-rugs, and demi-wolves, are clept
All by the name of dogs: the valu'd file
Distinguishes the swift, the slow, the subtle,
The housekeeper, the hunter, every one
According to the gift which bounteous Nature
Hath in him clos'd; whereby he does receive
Particular addition, from the bill
That writes them all alike . . .

— Shakespeare. *Macbeth*. Act III. Scene 1. c.1606.

Introduction

The epigraph indicates the value that has been historically attached to subtlety of distinctions in the language or lexicon of information retrieval systems. In this respect, the passage anticipates the principle formulated in modern discussions of indexing and classification that the value of an index term lies in its discriminatory power. In this principle, and in its historical anticipation, there is a strong, although largely unnoticed, contrast with the assumption of information retrieval research, particularly experimental information retrieval research, that the performance of an information retrieval system is to be measured by its capacity to deliver relevant records in response to deliberately articulated queries.

The concern here is, then, with whether the central principle embodied in the practice and theory of classification and indexing can yield more satisfying design and evaluative criteria for information retrieval systems than those that have been characteristically assumed in information retrieval research. Two paradigms have been distinguished in information retrieval research, the cognitive and the physical, but they share the assumption of the value of delivering relevant records (Belkin and Vickery, 1985, 114; Ellis, 1984, 19). For the purposes of the discussion here, they can be considered as a single, if heterogeneous, paradigm, linked if not united, by this common assumption.

The contrasting paradigm implicitly embodied in classification and indexing may finally be incommensurable with that of information retrieval research, with disputes not logically resolvable within either paradigm. The approach taken in this paper will be to suggest.

- That an alternative principle involving discriminatory power has been held, implicitly and explicitly, in a number of largely separate discourses.
- That the cumulative effect of recognizing this is to indicate more viable and productive criteria for designing, using, and evaluating information retrieval systems.
- And, finally, that the classical tradition of information retrieval research can itself be assimilated to the new model.

In this final respect, the development proposed here is an exemplar of scientific development in which discarded paradigms are absorbed into developing ones, as special cases.

The discourses in which an alternative principle for the design and evaluation of information retrieval systems can be discovered and that are to be covered here are.

- An emerging, although rather isolated and discontinuous, strand of information retrieval research.
- Discussions of the accepted principles of classification and indexing.

- Giambattista Vico's critique of Aristotelian principles and categories for classification.
- And, most crucially, ordinary language discussion of information systems.

This chapter will review information retrieval research, taking the liberty of conflating distinguishable aspects for the purposes of a higher level discussion, and then indicate that an alternative principle for evaluation can be found in the discourses identified. The value of the alternative model developed will be explored. In conclusion, it will be suggested that the alternative principle and criteria developed can have liberating effect, allowing theory and practice to interact, and that a productive transformation of the field has been indicated.

Alternative Paradigms

Information retrieval research

Information retrieval research, particularly in the experimental tradition emerging in the 1950s in Britain and North America, has taken as its founding assumption the principle that an ideal information system should deliver all (and possibly only all) the records relevant to a given information need. In order to evaluate information systems in relation to this desired end, or variations on it, various steps were taken: relevance was stabilized and quantified, sometimes being reduced to a binary or dichotomous variable; and measures of precision and recall, which depend on the prior stabilization of relevance, were developed. More recent research has questioned the validity of aspects of this paradigm, although more frequently with reference to its subsidiary concepts (relevance and information need) and derived measures (precision and recall) than with regard to its founding assumption.

The adequacy of the concept of relevance employed in information retrieval research has been questioned. Experiments substitute a measurable phenomenon, relevance as constructed under artificial conditions, for an unmeasurable one, relevance under operational conditions, but fail to demonstrate that there is an adequate correlation between the two. Most disturbingly, it has been suggested that operational relevance is fluid, influenced by intention, context, and other documents seen or read, and simply not amenable to stabilization or, further, quantification (Ellis, 1984; 1996).

The classical measures of precision and recall are also rendered increasingly artificial by the high degree of interactivity enabled by recent information technology developments. How, when searching a CD-ROM database, is the final set of records to be isolated except by a process whose very arbitrariness invalidates it as a component of a measure of system performance (Warner, 1992)? High interactivity, and unmediated searching, also reduces the need for a query to be fully articulated in advance of searching. There has also been a realization that a deliberately stated query (which can be distinguished from an information need or assertion of relevance) may be a methodological requirement for controlled experiment, but is not intrinsic to the information seeking situation (Heine, 1980) and that it is possible to search without verbalizing an information need.

The classic information retrieval paradigm, and the concepts and measures associated with it, could be preserved but only at the cost of increasing its distance from more realistic information seeking situations. It may be that not only are the classical concepts and measures both becoming and being recognized as increasingly artificial but that the founding assumption — that a system should deliver all (and only all) the relevant records should be re-examined. What is required, then, is not questioning of concepts with the paradigm but of its founding assumption, turning what has been received as a given into an object of enquiry.

To some extent, this has begun to occur within information retrieval research. The subtlety and complexity of information retrieval has been recognized (Swanson, 1988). Most specifically, the principle of exploratory capability, the ability to explore and make discriminations between representations of objects, has been suggested as the fundamental design principle for information retrieval systems (Ellis, 1984; 1996).

On a subjective level, this can be supported by introspection: that what I desire from an information retrieval system is not a possibly mysterious transformation of a query into a set of records, but a means of enlarging my capacity for informed choice between the representation of objects within the given universe of discourse. Such an enhanced capacity for informed choice broadly corresponds to exploratory capability. It could also be regarded as analogous to a sense of cognitive control over, or ability to discriminate between, representations of objects.

One example, which may be fictional in a double sense, can be given of the need for enhanced discriminatory power. At one point in time, a researcher might wish to distinguish the private individual, Samuel Langhorne Clemens, from the author, Mark Twain (perhaps out of interest in his copyright disputes or in his brother's, Orion Clemens's, activities as Secretary of the Nevada Territory). What would be valuable for this purpose would be a system that did not conflate these two distinguishable aspects of the individual but enabled them to be differentiated. At a later point in time, the same researcher might be interested in information on Mark Twain and Samuel Clemens considered as single entity. An information retrieval system should then be able to differentiate and to link together the occurrences of these different names, as required.

In conclusion, the assumption that it is desirable to obtain all, and possibly only all, the records relevant to a given query can be rejected in favor of the alternative principle of exploratory capability or enhanced capacity for informed choice. Introspection supported the value of exploratory capability. Its appeal as an alternative to the established information retrieval paradigm could be strengthened if it could be found, even if only implicitly or in analogous forms, in other, independently developed, discourses.

Principle of indexing and classification

An acknowledged principle of indexing and classification is that the value of a term is its discriminatory power. By discriminatory power is understood the ability to partition and select from the objects represented within the given universe of discourse. What particular terms or methods of classification are appropriate will vary with the area of discourse and the focus of interest: most obviously, a factor that differentiates one set of objects from another will not serve to discriminate within either set of objects. Discriminatory power is again analogous to exploratory capability, or, more accurately, a critical factor in enabling progressive and controlled exploration.

Vico's critique of Aristotelian classification

A strong, and highly significant, analogue to exploratory capability can be found in Vico's critique of Aristotle. Aristotle's philosophy, as well as being a direct and indirect source for subsequent understandings of genus, species, specific difference, synonymy and equivalence, involved, in some of its aspects, a systematic method of enquiry in order to classify an object. An enquirer was required to ask a series of questions: Does the thing exist? What is it? How big is it? What is its quality? and the like. This method of enquiry was subjected to an incisive critique by Vico:

> Aristotle's *Categories* and *Topics* are completely useless if one wants to find something new in them. One turns out to be a Llull or Kircher and becomes like a man who knows the alphabet, but cannot arrange the letters to read the great book of nature. But if these tools were considered the indices and ABC's of inquiries about our problem (of certain knowledge) so that we might have it fully surveyed, nothing would be more fertile for research. (Vico, 1988, 100-01)

The last clause of that critique deserves emphasis, "nothing would be more fertile for research." The rigidity of the method is avoided, while some of its techniques are retained, and it is transformed into a systematic and effective means for enhancing knowledge of an object. Analogously, while rejecting the rigid transformation of a query into a set of records assumed as desirable in information retrieval research, similar techniques can be used to explore the domain of discourse covered by the information retrieval system.

A further supporting analogue can be found in the fictional rather than discursive treatment of rigid classifications in Dickens's *Hard Times*. The logical distinctions exemplified in Bitzer's definition of a horse — "Quadruped. Graminivorous. Forty teeth, namely twenty-four grinders, four eye-teeth, and twelve incisive . . . Age known by marks in mouth." (Dickens, 1989, 6) — which does resemble nineteenth-century taxonomies for the horse, themselves influenced by the Aristotelian method of definition by genus and species, are presented as harsh (Warner, 1994, 106-8). Outside the restricting enclosure of the town, a different metaphor for knowledge is discernible:

> They walked on across the fields and down the shady lanes, sometimes getting over a fragment of a fence so rotten that it dropped at a touch of the foot, sometimes passing near a wreck of bricks and beams overgrown with grass, marking the site of deserted works. They followed paths and tracks, however slight. (Dickens, 1989, 353)

The value of an information system could then be the ability it offers discriminatingly to follow "paths and tracks, however slight." Classification schemes themselves (and their analogues in thesaural relations among indexing terms) can then be received not as fixed models of stable entities but as valuable exploratory devices.

Ordinary discourse

Ordinary, particularly informal spoken, discussion of information systems is simultaneously highly significant and difficult to produce as evidence. Evaluative criteria may be implied rather than explicitly articulated. Yet when a searcher complains that it is difficult to control the number of records retrieved, a principle of discriminatory power is being invoked. More explicitly, one spoken response to an earlier version of this paper was: "that's the basis (an enhanced capacity for informed choice) on which people use systems anyway."

Summary

Similarities in themes and principles enunciated or implied have been revealed in largely separate discourses, emerging in information retrieval research, implied in discussions of principles of indexing and classification, made explicit in Vico's critique of Aristotelian methods of investigation, and present, in partly unarticulated form, in ordinary discourse. The mode of expression varies, but an enhanced capacity for informed choice, for effective discrimination, or for cognitive control was discovered to be valued in all the discourses adduced. Independent agreement with an emerging and rather isolated theme in information retrieval research, of exploratory capability, offers support for replacing the established emphasis on the delivery of relevant records with such a principle for the design and use of information systems. In some respects, possibly through the influence of practices of indexing and classification and of ordinary discourse understandings, working systems may offer exploratory capability and productive interaction. In Vico's terms, practical understanding has been in advance of theoretical articulation.

Evaluative Model

Endorsing the principle of enhanced capacity for informed choice can have a liberating effect, revealing the intratheoretic nature of many disputes within the classic tradition of information retrieval research: it offers the possibility of a deeper understanding of relevance; enables a mutually informing relation between practice and theory; restores man as artificer as a user of information systems rather the cipher of information retrieval research; and can enable the development of more satisfying evaluative criteria.

Disputes over the validity of constructs demanded for retrieval system evaluation in the classic tradition of information retrieval research, for instance whether deliberately contrived relevance judgments are adequately correlative with real world judgments, can now be regarded as intratheoretic, connected with the theoretical framework imposed, not inherent in the process of information retrieval and not necessarily contributing to an understanding of those processes. In some respects, the construction imposed by the research paradigm may even have inhibited development of understanding of its chosen domain of study. For instance, the methodological need to reduce relevance to assessments, possibly open to quantification, and stable over time, may have inhibited exploration of its many possible dimensions. Some dissenting discussions have insisted on its complex and multifaceted nature (Watson and others, 1973; P. Wilson, 1973).

A mutually informing and productive relation between theory and practice can be developed. For instance, the practical experience of those indexing procedures or retrieval algorithms that enhance exploratory capability in specified circumstances can inform theoretical development and system design and modification. The divorce of information retrieval research from practice has been noted and sometimes regretted, although less often explained. Now the practical understanding embodied in working systems can be recognized and theoretically developed.

The further question then also arises as to whether accepting the principle of exploratory capability has practical implications in terms of the indexing procedures or algorithms for searching to be adopted. An immediate response would be that it does not necessarily have unambiguous practical implications: That the particular indexing procedures and algorithms to be used will be critically dependent on the purpose and context of retrieval, including the cost of indexing and retrieval. Crucially for continuity of systems development, techniques identical with or analogous to those currently developed may be used to different ends. It should also be noted that the Boolean logic used in many retrieval systems, does, under certain conditions, have the advantage of relative transparency to the searcher (the distinction between techniques and ends is more fully developed in chapter 6). The objection that it is an ineffective way of transforming an information need into a set of relevant records is no longer tenable. It could still be objected that for some applications, for instance with heterogeneous written material without humanly assigned index terms, it gives inadequate control over the representations within the universe of discourse.

A deeper effect is to restore man as an artificer and to recognize the subtlety of the processes involved information retrieval. Rather than being subjected to retrieval process beyond immediate control, the searcher is presented with an enhanced capacity for choice and for making recalled sets. The new, and historically unprecedented, potential for enhanced forms of knowing of existing textual material can then be productively explored. For instance, the unrivalled opportunity offered by full text database for exploring the semantic mutability of written word forms with different contexts can be pursued.

More detailed evaluative criteria could be developed from the central evaluative principle of enhanced choice, partly by drawing on the understandings already developed in discussions of classification. Yet it should be recognized that quantitative comparative measures are unlikely to result. Once the diversity of contexts for information retrieval is recognized, the idea of a single, generally applicable approach to system design, or a single comparative measure of system performance, becomes severely questionable. The best outcome that can reasonably be expected from research and from reflection on practice is a better understanding of the process of information retrieval, which can then be used either to design better information systems or to maker more effective use of existing systems.

Conclusion

Replacing the emphasis on the delivery of relevant records with a stress on exploratory capability or cognitive control as a design and use principle for information retrieval can have a liberating effect. It yields more satisfying evaluative criteria while preserving a strong continuity with previous work, particularly in recognizing the utility of developed information retrieval techniques. Theory and practice, rather than being separate or even antagonistic, are enabled to inform each other. The discourses, of philosophy, classification and ordinary discussion, from which the new principle has been drawn, can be brought further to bear upon information retrieval, transforming it into a human science and recognizing its subtlety and significance. A minor, although significant, relief, is liberation from the obligation to read work in the classic information retrieval paradigm, except for the emerging signs of self-questioning.

The transformation advocated in this paper resembles, in some respects, a mathematical revolution and can also be seen as an example of scientific progress. Classically fundamental transformations of mathematics have preserved the form while modifying the interpretation (Ramsey, 1990) (see also chapter 6); analogously, information retrieval techniques have been preserved but adapted to a new end. More broadly, it has been argued that a discipline exhibits the history of a true science if its earlier stages can be seen as special cases, from the perspective of its subsequent development (Roberts, 1982): in this context, the automatic transformation of a query into a set of records can be seen as a possible support for informed choice, valuable in certain sets of circumstances. Rather than, as D. R. Swanson indicated, "Waiting for Godot, we fail to grasp what is now within reach" (Swanson, 1988, 97), we can begin to explore the potential for improving human interaction with recorded knowledge.

Chapter 6

Meta- and Object-Language for Information Retrieval Research: Proposal for a Distinction

The distinction meta:object has become increasingly familiar from the contrast between metadata and the objects described (Demsey and Heerey, 1998), although the term object-data is not necessarily used. In that context, the term *metadata* is used to indicate a concise and deliberately encoded description of a set of objects. In wider, although not necessarily ordinary, usage, a metalanguage is congruently understood as a language that supplies terms for the analysis of an object-language or as a system of propositions about other propositions (Oxford, 1989).

Partly forgotten antecedents to the meta:object distinction can be discovered, in different disciplinary contexts. *Within* information retrieval research, analysis of the structure of indexing vocabularies has differentiated the *metalanguage* of index terms from the *object-language* of the documents described. The metalanguage could be a thesaurus or classification scheme, with human application of constituent terms to objects, or could be algorithmically generated from the object-language. The distinction was found valuable for revealing commonalities between apparently differing index language structures (Gardin, 1973). A fuller antecedent, which is also more immediately relevant to the purpose here, is provided by formal logic. There, a distinction has been made between the verbal *metalanguage* of discussion and interpretation and the symbolic *object-language*, which has been found to yield advantages in analytical clarity (Bochenski, 1961). Information retrieval research has been recognized as being in a conceptually confused state (Ellis, 1996). A comparable gain to the clarity obtained in formal logic could be derived from applying an analogous distinction to information retrieval research, considered as a whole, and not simply to items of concern within it.

Discussions about information retrieval can be regarded as a *metalanguage* and algorithmic transformations carried out within information retrieval systems as an *object-language*. Such a distinction between the metalanguage of discussion and the object-language of system transformations can be discovered *in* information retrieval research but has not yet been fully known *to* it. From this perspective, it is particularly disturbing that a technique or aspect of the object-language, non-Boolean searching, should have been raised to a research end (Belkin and Croft, 1987; Ellis, 1990).

Rendering the distinction between meta- and object-language explicit can enable information retrieval research to draw upon discourses, particularly formal logic, in which some of the issues it encounters have already been addressed. It can also provide the basis for constructing a simpler metalanguage than that developed in classic information retrieval research, with a sharp reduction in the number of entities distinguished and in its artificiality, while preserving the intellectual labor embodied in object-language transformations. In preserving intellectual labor, the distinction would have strategic value, in economy of research effort, as well as enabling greater theoretical clarity.

This chapter will first review the distinction between a meta- and object-language in formal logic and indicate that an analogous distinction can be made for information retrieval research and systems. Intratheoretic distinctions currently embodied in the metalanguage of information retrieval research will be dissolved. The transformations possible in the object-language can then be accounted for by reference to the understandings established in formal logic. Finally, it will be concluded that the perspective developed allows a degree of freedom in selection of significant issues from the existing metalanguage of discussion and economy of research effort in carrying forward some of the algorithms developed for information retrieval system object-languages.

Meta- and Object-Language

In formal logic

The distinction of meta- from object-language in formal logic is here understood as a distinction between the verbal language of commentary or discussion and the symbolic object-language. A critical source for the distinction is F. P. Ramsey's work of the 1920s. First, in a critique of the *Principia Mathematica*, a contrast is made between the ideas and the propositions of mathematics:

> There are really two distinct categories of things of which an account must be given — the ideas or concepts of mathematics, and the propositions of mathematics. This distinction is neither artificial nor unnecessary, for the great majority of writers on the subject have concentrated their attention on the explanation of one or other of these categories, and erroneously supposed that a satisfactory explanation of the other would immediately follow. (Ramsey, 1990, 165)

The distinction made by Ramsey was later rephrased as a distinction between the object-language of a symbolic logic and the metalanguage of discourse about that object-language, although Ramsey himself does not use these terms. The distinction has been generally, although not universally, accepted in formal logic and is recognized to have a simplifying effect. In this context, we are not concerned with the final validity of the distinction but with the example of its clarifying effect (Bochenski, 1961, 402; Kneale and Kneale, 1962, 664-665) (1).

The intention here is to propose an analogous distinction for information retrieval, between its ideas or concepts and its propositions or algorithmic transformations. The distinction can be made to offer a basis for a comparable gain in analytical clarity for information retrieval research. It may also prevent independent rediscovery of analogous issues, of which there are already signs, most notably in the separate development of the understanding of the primitive operations of information retrieval (Buckland and Plaunt, 1994) and of the object-language of formal logic. Many writers on information retrieval have also confused an explanation of the concepts of information retrieval with an explanation of its propositions or object-language.

For information retrieval

The metalanguage of discussion about information retrieval systems can, then, be differentiated from the object-language of the transformations carried out within information retrieval systems. The *value*, as distinct from the *possibility*, of the distinction would depend on its clarifying effect and strategic significance and these will be indicated here. Having differentiated meta- from object-language, dialectic interaction between them is then enabled.

The metalanguage of classic information retrieval research has characteristically, although not necessarily explicitly, displayed (Ellis, 1996; Harter and Hert, 1997) (2).

- A founding assumption
- Some central concepts subsidiary to that assumption
- Entities distinguished for evaluative purposes
- Some derived measures

Distinctions between its founding assumption, central concepts, and other aspects have not always been acknowledged and have sometimes been confused, but can be made to emerge more clearly here.

Founding assumption

The founding assumption has been of the value of delivering all, and possibly only all, the records (or other objects) relevant to an information need and this has only occasionally been questioned. This assumption has been held by the different paradigms that have been distinguished in information retrieval research, the cognitive and the physical (Ellis, 1992). Some recent research, finding antecedents in a rather isolated and discontinuous stream of information retrieval research, has rather advocated exploratory capability (Ellis, 1984), an enhanced capacity for informed choice (see chapter 5), or evaluation and filtering of material (P. Wilson, 1996a), as fundamental principles for the design and use of information systems. The choice between the established and the more recently proposed founding principles might not be logically resolvable within the classic information retrieval paradigm, but the principle of informed choice has been valued implicitly in ordinary discourse discussions of information systems, as a principle of cataloguing and indexing, and, explicitly, in some philosophical disputes (see chapter 5), and will be endorsed here.

Central concepts

Some central concepts are explicitly invoked within the founding assumption of classic information retrieval research, particularly information need and relevance, and these have been more developed and questioned. To some extent, the central subsidiary concept of relevance has been confused with the founding assumption of information retrieval research. In particular, the idea, that relevance, and not measures derived from the prior stabilization of relevance, has been the criterion for system evaluation, has been reiterated. Further confusions have been between understanding relevance and searching for a unified concept, and between the intratheoretic and possible ordinary discourse senses of relevance (Saracevic, 1976). From the perspective here, information need and relevance can be retained as concepts whose development need not be restrained or made rigid by the founding assumption or by the methodological requirements of system evaluation.

Entities for evaluative purposes

For practical system evaluation, particularly in the experimental tradition, relevance has been stabilized, some entities, such as the query, and derived measures, particularly precision and recall, introduced. Relevance has been reduced to a binary variable, conceived primarily, although not always explicitly, as a relation between a document and a query. It should be noted that the stabilization of relevance, its reduction to a binary variable (although degrees of relevance have been admitted) and to a document:query relation, are contingent on the evaluative techniques adopted, not on the founding assumption of information retrieval research or on relevance as a concept. A verbal query articulated in advance of searching has usually been a methodological requirement for system evaluation. As such, it has been recognized as intratheoretic (Heine, 1980), although the significance of this recognition has only recently been appreciated. The alternative suggested to the query, the assertion of relevance (Heine, 1980), might prove equally artificial, although it has been used as a beginning point of departure from the received paradigm (Warner, 1992).

Derived measures

Measures, such as precision and recall, dependent on the prior stabilization and reduction of relevance, and on the introduction of artificial entities, such as the query, have then been employed in system evaluation. Other measures, for instance, utility, have been proposed, without necessarily being fully explicit about the assumptions, concepts, and entities shared with the construction of precision and recall.

Critiques have convincingly argued that the reduction of relevance from a concept to a relation, the introduction of artificial entities and of derived measures, have inhibited, rather than assisted, the growth of understanding of information seeking and retrieval (Ellis, 1984; Warner, 1992).

If the founding assumption of classic information retrieval research is discarded, little may be left of subsidiary and contingent concepts, entities, and derived measures to be carried forward. It may have to be conceded that the metalanguage of information retrieval research as inhibited, rather than advanced, understanding of the activities with which it is concerned (Ellis, 1984). Discussion of relevance as an intellectual construct, rather than as a query:document relation, athwart rather than within the dominant research tradition, for instance (Watson and others, 1973; Swift, Winn, and Bramer, 1977; P. Wilson, 1973), will still be valuable. Replacing the founding assumption of the value of delivering relevant records with an emphasis on enhancing the capacity for informed choice, or exploratory capability, enables the assumed antithesis with relevance to be dissolved. Relevance can rather be regarded as a significant dimension of informed choice or exploratory capability and may itself have further dimensions. Similarly, a query, and even more a fully verbally articulated query, made in advance of searching is revealed as an intratheoretic construct, connected with the methodological demands of evaluation, not intrinsic to information seeking. The effect of this transformation of the metalanguage should be liberating, giving full priority to purpose over technique, enabling a simpler and more flexible metalanguage, with a fuller correspondence to practice, and eliminating unnecessary intratheoretic entities.

Object-language

Regarding transformations within information retrieval systems as an object-language can yield analytical and strategic advantages in three related respects.

- First, the transformations possible within the object-language can be related to understandings established in formal logic and automata theory;
- Secondly, dialectic engagement between meta- and object-language is enabled, while recognizing their mutual distinction;

- And, thirdly, as part of that dialectic, the intellectual labor embodied in developed object-languages can be selectively carried forward, freed from the constraining assumptions of the existing metalanguage.

Relation to automata theory and formal logic

A recently formulated view regards the primitive operations of information retrieval searching as functions that operate on data objects, with the functions reducible to transformation, sorting, and partitioning. The level of granularity at which these functions and objects are viewed can be adapted to the purposes of investigation (Buckland and Plaunt, 1994). In this analysis, there is a strong, although as yet publicly unnoticed, analogy, if not identity, with the understandings established in formal logic and mathematics since the 1920s, that the operations of mathematics consist of the writing, erasure, and substitution of symbols. Similar understandings have been developed in automata theory, partly independently and at a later date, in which, similarly, different levels of granularity are permissible, for exposition and understanding (Warner, 2001d). An established body of knowledge could, then, be drawn upon to address the compelling task of how information systems work (Blair and Maron, 1990), at least on the syntactic level. In addition, interactive searching, or searching of a system embodied in a fixed medium such as paper or microform, could be regarded as analogous to nondeterminism, in the specific technical sense of human interaction being required to move an automaton from an ambiguous or halting state, with the possibility of semantic, and not simply syntactic, transformations (Warner, 1994, 77-92). In terms of their role of information systems in human communication and contribution to knowledge, a richer and fuller metalanguage, for which contributing antecedents can be found, needs to be constructed (Smithson, 1994). Simultaneously, it must be acknowledged that this metalanguage is likely to be less open to precise logical formulations than the object-language.

Meta- and object-language

Dialectic engagement between meta- and object-language, giving full priority to purpose over technique, is also enabled. If the principle of enlarged informed choice is taken as the fundamental aim for information systems, the automatic transformation of a query into a set of relevant records can be regarded as a special case or as techniques that can, under certain circumstances, be used to assist informed choice. The real world context of direct and opportunity costs of searching, considered within the enlarged metalanguage, can also be considered. Similar algorithms developed as part of existing object-languages may be used for different purposes, within a contrasting metalinguistic framework.

Preservation of intellectual labor

This distinction enables the intellectual labor embodied in existing object-languages to be carried forward, giving a strategic advantage in economy of research development. One specific, and significant, example of a factor that could be produced by similar techniques or transformations in the object-language, but that has already been valued for different ends, would be offered by discriminatory power: in discussions of human indexing, it has been valued, in effect although not necessarily explicitly, for the help it gives to enlarging informed choice (Collins, 1998, 45; see also chapter 5); in classic information retrieval research, it has been regarded as a factor assisting the automatic partitioning of documents (Rijsbergen, 1979, 29 and 76). Sophisticated algorithms in the object-languages, developed for one purpose, could then be adapted to different purposes.

Conclusion

Distinguishing meta- from object-language for information retrieval research has yielded analytic clarity. A partial synthesis of apparently antithetical viewpoints, of an emphasis on developing algorithms to meet a conception of relevance as a document query relation with a valuing of informed choice, has been enabled. More broadly, this could be regarded as a particular aspect of a possible synthesis between computational and document traditions in information science (Buckland, 1999). The synthesis is only partial in that the metalanguage of classic information retrieval research had to be largely discarded. A specific further task would be to establish which object-languages assist particular metalinguistic purposes, for instance high or low discrimination between documents or document records.

A triple strategic value can be attached to the position constructed, in terms of its congruence with real world developments, enabling the intellectual reintegration of information retrieval research, and preservation of intellectual labor. Real world, as distinct from experimental, Internet search engines are using object-languages derived from information retrieval research while users may be adapting those systems to other ends. Ordinary discourse discussions about information systems would strongly suggest that this focuses, in an implied manner, on the possibility of informed choice (see chapter 5). The intellectual labor embodied in existing object-languages has not been discarded. Their adaptation to different ends indicates the interpretative flexibility of the artifacts in use (see chapter 2), but informed choice could be transformed into a deliberate design principle (and there are signs that this is occurring). The metalanguage of information retrieval research can be reintegrated with the human sciences, with significant antecedents recovered, for instance from philosophy and discussions of the value of classification (see chapter 5). For the object-language, existing understandings in formal logic and automata theory have been made relevant, with the aim of preventing diseconomies in independent rediscovery.

To attempt to demand observance of the meta:object distinction within information retrieval research would show a misunderstanding of the way scholarly communities change, characteristically by a failure to attract recruits rather than by internal changes of conviction (Kuhn, 1970). Yet there are forces discernible that may assist the transformation of the distinction from one *discoverable in* to one *known to* information retrieval, particularly the diffusion of systems or object-languages beyond the communities that constructed them. In particular, since the early 1990s the object-languages of classic information retrieval research have diffused widely beyond the communities that developed them and that, to some extent, controlled their interpretation, with the development of Internet search engines. In this sense, information retrieval research has finally extensively influenced practice, having previously had only limited real-world influence (Ellis, 1990; Ellis and Vasconceloss, 1999). Users of such systems may be operating within an implied metalanguage, for instance stressing informed choice, different from that originally conceived and this may assist the development of an explicit distinction. In summary, the distinction is congruent with, although not explicit in, powerful and developing real-world forces.

Dialectic engagement with the existing meta- or object language, or languages, of classic information retrieval research has contrasting possibilities, for future development. It might be tempting to believe that the existing metalanguage could be transformed into an object for productive interaction, enabling the research effort embodied in it partly to be preserved. Yet with the theoretical rejection and practical erosion of its founding assumption (of the value of delivering all and possibly only all the relevant records in response to a query), this seems unlikely to be productive, even for subsidiary concepts, entities, and measures. Precision and recall can be retained, but in their ordinary discourse sense as dimensions of a search (embodied in a reference to a precision-oriented search), not as measures. In contrast, the intellectual labor embodied in the object-language can be preserved and carried forward, although adapted to different metalinguistic purposes. A similar strategic value, of congruence with real-world developments, can be attached to this position.

In conclusion, the application of the distinction between meta- and object-language to information retrieval research has yielded a significant gain in analytical clarity. Access to knowledge stored publicly is too significant an issue for the study of it to be dominated by computer technology and formal characterizations (Heine, 1983). The historical dominance of such formal characterizations suggests that the object-language, and the forms of thinking associated with the object-language, have been taken for the whole. The distinction proposed here at least allows us effectively to discriminate between a significant component and the entirety of meta- and object-language.

Notes

1. A partial, although not fully acknowledged, ambiguity exists with regard to the understanding of a metalanguage in formal logic. In some instances, it is understood as the verbal language of commentary and interpretation, in contradistinction to the symbolic object-language (Bochenski, 1961). In other cases, and possibly more strongly in late-20th-century logic, it is also understood as a symbolic language that can be used to speak about a symbolic object-language (McGee, 1998; Moore 1998). Where the metalanguage is understood as the verbal language of commentary, it historically emerged from a distinction between contradictions expressed in symbols and in words, which was later assimilated to the meta:object distinction. Understood as the verbal language of

commentary, it has had the greater relevant clarifying effect and this will therefore be the primary understanding and focus here.

2. The literature of classic information retrieval research is extensive and reference to reviews of the literature is made in the interests of economy.

Chapter 7

Forms of Labor in Information Systems

A high degree of discursive coherence is characteristically demanded for scholarly communication, in written and published form. Discursive coherence, and the finished appearance of a printed product, can give the illusion of closure to a dialogic process. Greater informality is allowed for oral presentations. In this context, I wish to take advantage of the chapter's inheritance from its original electronic publication, capable of combining oral and written elements (see chapter 4), and present observations aphoristically, but still permanently and with a definite rhetorical structure.

The justification for this mode of presentation lies in the developing nature of the field (consciousness is lagging behind reality). For:

> Another error . . . is the over early and peremptory reduction of knowledge into arts and methods; from which time commonly sciences receive small or no augmentation . . . knowledge, while it is in aphorisms and observations, it is in growth: but when it once is comprehended in exact methods, it may perchance be further polished and illustrate and accommodated for use and practice; but it increaseth no more in bulk and substance. (Bacon, 1973, 32)

The knowledge embodied in this chapter then remains open to growth.

The "exact methods" referred to by Bacon are often associated with writing, most famously in Bacon's own observation "writing [maketh] an exact man" (Bacon, 1985, 209). Exactness has also tended to attract cultural prestige. Yet reservations on the value of exactness can be found (Warner, 2001a), even, as here, for the development of sciences.

Exactness will also occur as a substantive theme of the discussion, particularly in connection with the possibilities and limitations of syntactic semiotic labor (a concept to be developed and explained).

Technology as a Human Construction

The view of technology as a radical human construction (explored in chapter 2) will be taken as the basis for subsequent discussion. The idea of technology, capable of performing autonomous labor, as industrial technology would have been broadly true of Marx's historical period:

> Only in large-scale industry has man succeeded in making the product of his past labour, labour which has already been objectified, perform gratuitous service on a large scale, like a force of nature. (Marx, 1976, 510)

Information technologies for message transmission were increasingly diffused from the mid-1860s and these are acknowledged by Marx, in a later passage that takes an inclusive view of communication:

> the last fifty years have brought a revolution that is comparable only with the industrial revolution of the second half of the last century. On land the Macadamized road has been replaced by the railway, while at sea the slow and irregular sailing ship has been driven into the background by the rapid and regular steamer line; the whole earth has been girded by telegraph cables. (Marx, 1981, 164)

The industrial technologies of the nineteenth century, such as the steamhammer "that can crush a man or pat an egg-shell" (Dickens, 1946, 150), would have contained control mechanisms for variation in force, even if such mechanisms are not fully acknowledged in the classic concept of the simple machine (Minsky, 1967, 7). Primitive logic machines, such as Jevons's logic piano, were also developed in the late nineteenth century (Gardner, 1958).

More recently, the Marxian conception of technology as a radical human construction has been extended to information technologies, understood, rather schematically, as a form of knowledge concerned with the transformation of signals from one form or medium into another (see chapter 2). From this perspective, the language, including the written language, used by Marx can be seen as a cumulative creation of the "general intellect." Congruently with the growth of message transmission technologies, the late nineteenth century also witnessed the diffusion of nonverbal and abbreviated forms of writing, in logical notations, telegraphic codes, and shorthand.

The extension of a concept describing industrial technologies to include information technologies implies continuity from industrial to information societies, with both potentially subsumed under capitalism. Familiarly, within discussions of the information society, continuities are counterposed to disjunctions with industrial and capitalist eras (Webster, 1995a). A Marxian perspective can again be both novel and informative, in this context:

> It is not what is made but how, and by what instruments of labour, that distinguishes different economic epochs. . . . The writers of history have so far paid very little attention to the development of material production, which is the basis of all social life, and therefore of all real history. But prehistoric times at any rate have been classified on the basis on the investigations of natural science, rather than so-called historical research. Prehistory has been divided, according to the materials used to make tools and weapons, into the Stone Age, the Bronze Age and the Iron Age. (Marx, 1976, 286)

Developments in the instruments of informational labor must be acknowledged, with the computer, as a universal information machine, displacing calculation and, increasingly, writing by hand, as well as special purpose information machines. Yet an underlying and underpinning continuity also exists, strikingly revealed in the theoretical development of the computer from an account of mathematical operations as the writing, erasure, and substitution of symbols. It questionable whether modern information technologies constitute a transformation in material production rather than a significant addition. An understanding of information as a perspective rather than as a disjunction from preexisting forms of social organization is, then, preferred here (see chapter 1).

If we acknowledge continuities (while not denying contrasts), can we detect or construct an information dynamic that is continuous with the dynamic of capitalism?

Awakening of dead labor

Classically, living labor is required to reawaken the dead labor embodied in machinery and thereby to confer use- and exchange-value on inert stuff (Marx, 1976, 527; see chapter 2). The fictional or mythic analogue to this process is supplied by Frankenstein giving life to his creation:

> With an anxiety that almost amounted to agony, I collected the instruments of life around me that I might infuse a spark of being into the lifeless thing that lay at my feet. It was already one in the morning; the rain pattered dismally against the panes, and my candle was nearly burnt out, when, by the glimmer of the half-extinguished light, I saw the dull yellow eye of the creature open; it breathed hard, and a convulsive motion agitated its limbs. (Shelley, 1998, 38-39)

The awakening of dead physical or industrial labor by human action has analogies in the use of information technologies, specifically, in one interpretation of nondeterminism in automata theory, where determinism is understood as the automatic transformations in the intervals between human intervention (regarded as nondeterminist).

An Information Dynamic

Can an information dialectic or dynamic then be constructed and detected in empirical developments?

Dialectics or dynamics have been constructed for other fields. For instance, in medicine a dialectic has been detected between the amelioration of known maladies and the consequential rise of enemies to health (Graham, 1999, 40). The fundamental dynamic of capitalism has been seen as the substitution of dead for living labor, with the aim of decreasing the current costs of production. This process of substitution yields benefits (teleologically, the historic role of capitalism):

> a permanent tendency to increase the social productivity of labour is the main civilizing by-product of capital accumulation, the main objective service which capitalism has rendered mankind. (Mandel, 1976, 60)

In bibliography, the desire of bibliographers to bring order out of chaos is continually frustrated and fed by the urge of the authors, including bibliographers, to publish.

To construct an information dynamic, partly continuous with the fundamental dynamic of capitalism and inclusive of the dialectic between order and chaos in bibliography, some distinctions must be made between forms of human intellectual labor.

Human intellectual labor

A distinction specific to intellectual labor, although it has analogues in physical labor, must be made between semantic and syntactic labor. A distinction derived from existing discussions, and there already partly applied to semiotic products, can be made between universal and communal labor.

Semantic and syntactic labor

Semantic labor is concerned with the content, meaning, or, in semiotic terms, the signified of messages. The intention of semantic labor may be the construction of further messages, for instance, a description of the original message or a dialogic response.

Syntactic labor is concerned with the form, expression, or signifier of the original message. Transformations operating on the form alone may produce further messages (classically, this would be exemplified in the logic formalized by Boole).

Both semantic and syntactic labor are expensive when directly performed by humans. Education, both formal and informal, has been regarded as constituting the production costs of intellectual labor (scholars will be acutely aware that exchange value of intellectual labor need not be directly commensurate with its production costs and that semiotic labor can be conducted in the leisure enabled by other forms of labor). The objects of semantic labor can become objects of syntactic labor when a process is modeled or formalized, although the opening quotation from Bacon would suggest a restricted possibility of further growth. Syntactic labor need not be simple: consider the complexity of logical systems, for instance (a nonconstructivist view of mathematics would admit the possibility of syntactically generating acceptable, but complex and previously unknown, statements).

A dual impulse to formalization, and to the diffusion of formalisms, can be detected. The cultural value of exactness may motivate attempts at formalization and positively influence their reception. The reduced labor involved in the operation of formalized processes (contrast direct multiplication with the use of logarithms) may impel both their construction and their diffusion. In their diffusion, formalizations renew the prestige of exactness and demonstrate the economic advantages of reduced labor.

The transition from oral to oral and written linguistic communication could be regarded as the opening possibility of a distinction between syntactic and semantic levels of consideration, when applied to human and social not mathematical, or, more narrowly, numerical domains.

Universal and communal labor

The distinction between universal and communal labor made by Marx can be recalled and developed:

> We must distinguish here, incidentally, between universal labour and communal labour. They both play their part in the production process, and merge into one another, but they are each different as well. Universal labour is all scientific work, all discovery and invention. It is brought about partly by the cooperation of men now living, but partly also by building on earlier work. Communal labour, however, simply involves the direct cooperation of individuals. (Marx, 1981, 199)

Universal labor, understood as science, discovery, and invention, could be regarded as an aspect of the general intellect that transforms the process of social life. Communal labor is crucial to the awakening and use of universal labor, both as embodied in technologies and written texts. In the narrative of Frankenstein, universal labor would be represented by the learning used by Frankenstein and by the instruments of life, and communal labor, here mediated through a single individual, in the application of that learning and those instruments.

With regard to "building on earlier work," disciplines are understood to differ in the extent to which they are cumulative. Disciplines marked by the extensive use of syntactic operations most obviously mathematics, are regarded as more strictly cumulative than the human sciences, and, even more the texts and artifacts studied in the human sciences (consider the reduction of Shannon's seminal work in 1938 on analogies between Boolean logic and switching circuits to material for secondary education, over the subsequent fifty years).

Empirical Application of Distinctions

Since the late nineteenth century, information technologies that can be used to perform syntactic labor have been increasingly developed. These technologies have been adapted to public domain information retrieval systems and have also influenced the development of copyright. I will consider information retrieval systems and copyright, but my further purpose is to suggest that distinctions between forms of labor, and the dynamic constructed, could inform understandings of other areas of information activity.

Information retrieval systems

I wish, in this context, to confine attention to system predominantly concerned with written language. Oral and nonverbal forms of graphic communication, which have undergone less clearly marked historically accumulated forms of coding, presented different issues for retrieval system design. Most obviously, they do not necessarily offer readily distinguishable syntactic units with potential semantic significance.

Two antithetical, if not always clearly distinguished, traditions can be detected in information retrieval system design and evaluation. The idea of query transformation, understood as the automatic transformation of a query into a set of relevant records, has been dominant in information retrieval theory. A principle of selection power has been valued in ordinary discourse, librarianship, and, to some extent, in practical system design and use. Philosophical antecedents to the idea of selection power can also be found (see chapter 4) (consider also the etymology of intelligence, from the Latin *inter-legere*, to choose between). The debate between query transformation and selection power may not be resolvable within either paradigm, but, in this context, I wish to take the privilege of assuming selection power as the founding principle for system design, evaluation, and use.

Selection power may be the design principle, but *selection labor* could be regarded as the primary concept, from which selection power is derived. Let us assume a resistance to labor (I note here a degree of congruence between Marx and Zipf) and that a relatively fixed quantity of selection labor is shared between system producer and searcher, with variation of the distribution between those poles.

Selection power is valued by a searcher as it reduces their selection labor (and an exhaustive serial search may not be a practical possibility). *Description labor* by the system producer tends to aim to increase the selection power of the searcher and reduce their selection labor (description labor is understood to include cataloguing, or document description, and classification, or subject categorization, incidentally revealing the congruence between their aims). The semantic and syntactic intellectual labor embodied in documents described is here treated as a given. The description labor of the system producer can contain elements of syntactic labor, for instance, transcription or transformation of the object-language of documents described into the metalanguage of index representations, and of semantic labor, for instance the application of thesaural terms derived from a controlled vocabulary or of cataloguing codes to the description of documents. In the nineteenth century, both syntactic and semantic labor might have involved continuous human intervention (consider the creation of *Palmer's Index to The Times* and the primarily syntactic labor of transcribing newspaper headlines as index entries); in modern practice, syntactic labor is delegated to humanly constructed technologies, and, accordingly, human intellectual labor becomes almost exclusively semantic.

Universal labor is understood as information technologies, in both their hardware and software aspects, and communal labor as the awakening or use of those technologies, including semantic record description.

A diagram may clarify these distinctions (see Figure 7.2). The classification of systems from highly to loosely structured is tautological in that it is derived from the objects described and the framework of description, but may still be informative.

The *Financial Times,* in its various searchable manifestations, provides a peculiarly pure example of the distinction between syntactic and semantic labor. It is available as a web resource without payment at the point of use, with largely syntactically generated search facilities that operate on identifiable units of the source. It is also available with additional description, generated from human semantic labor (which could be syntactically assisted), from a number of vendors. For instance, the Dialog available file labels articles by geopolitical region and product/industry names, including the North American Industry Classification System (NAICS) code. Direct payment at point of use is made for the resources that embody additional semantic labor. The continuity of such sources is market testimony to readiness to pay for

Figure 7.1. Forms of labor in information retrieval systems.

Type of System	Information System	Universal Intellectual Labor	Communal Intellectual Labor		Selection Work of Searcher
Highly Structured	OCLC *WorldCat*, *Financial Times* with added indexing	Information technologies	System construction and maintenance (search engine or directory structure)	Record creation (standards for cataloguing and subject description): human semantic work	Reduced
Medium Structured	*BUBL* (Internet directory), *Lycos UK*	Algorithms for automatic (syntactic) processing and indexing of written language		Description of resources; creation and maintenance of directory structure: human semantic work	Intermediate
Loosely Structured	*Google* (Internet search engine), Newspaper web site, *Palmer's Index to The Times*			Automatically generated descriptions	Intensive

additional selection power (and further evidence for the congruence of the concept with ordinary discourse understandings and everyday practice). Provision of both types of resource involves similar access to the universal labor embodied in information technologies and comparable communal labor to reinvigorate those technologies.

The costs of human labor in description can be more broadly considered. For instance the costs of creating a catalogue record to the standards required for *World Cat* are in the order of U.S.$40. The labor in description may contain syntactic elements, for instance, in transcription, but will be predominantly semantic. Costs of syntactic labor, by contrast, in storage, manipulation, and transmission of records have diminished historically, and continue to diminish, as communal human labor is transformed into universal labor. Labor invested in record description increases the selection power and reduces the selection labor of the searcher.

Returning to the overall schema embodied in the diagram, we can see that producers of information systems, from highly to loosely structured, have comparable access to universal intellectual labor, embodied in the language they use, and, specifically, in the information technologies available. Comparable, although contrasting, levels of communal labor would be required for system design and maintenance. Strikingly different levels of direct human labor are given to document description: for records in library and union catalogues, intense semantic labor is needed (whose intensity could be related to the exactness required); for Internet directories, selection and description of resources, although to less exacting standards; for Internet search engines, very little, if any, additional semantic labor. The communal labor invested in the description of resources reduces the selection labor of the searcher (with both forms of labor reflecting the high costs of direct human employment).

The model can be validated, from macro- to microlevels. At a macro-level, syntactically based systems proliferate (consider the variety of Internet search engines), while semantically enriched systems, such as *World Cat*, may occupy unique market positions. Simultaneously, their search facilities, products of universal labor, are converging in appearance and power. At an intermediate level, the function of library cooperatives has changed over time, moving along the horizontal axis of the diagram, from adapting universal labor to a concern with sharing the descriptive labor of cataloguing (from awakening Frankenstein's monster to distributing its limbs). At a more microlevel, the relative costs of communal and universal labor, considered in relation to market demand, form the decision framework for the conversion of historical resources from paper to electronic form (including *Palmers Index to The Times*). For information retrieval systems, the communal labor invested in description at production reduces the labor required at use (proposals for coding in the semantic web could be understood as part of this dialectic). The distribution of direct human labor between producer and searcher may depend on the nature of the market for the product.

Information retrieval systems, then, can be seen to exhibit the fundamental dynamic of capitalism, the substitution of dead for living labor, although semiotic rather than physical labor. The specific, and already known, dynamic of bibliography between order and chaos is accentuated. Chaos is further enabled by the reduced costs of making information public. Possibilities for order are enhanced by the availability of delegated syntactic labor (although the limitations of such labor are becoming painfully known). The resources giving control themselves contribute to overall disorder (consider Search Engine Watch, at http://www.searchenginewatch.com/ in relation to Theodore Besterman's *A World Bibliography of Bibliographies* and classic concerns with bibliographic proliferation).

Copyright

I wish here to review the striking reversal of the labor or "sweat of the brow" theory of copyright by the *Feist* judgment of 1991 and to suggest that a similar dynamic, between living and dead labor, underlies the reversal and its date of occurrence.

The classic liberal justification for intellectual property, including copyright, given in the U.S. Constitution, can be recalled:

> The Congress shall have Power . . . To promote the Progress of Science and useful Arts, by securing for limited Times to Authors and Inventors the exclusive Right to their respective Writings and Discoveries. (Constitution, 1789)

Discussions of copyright have tended to refer to the balance between the two ends of promoting science and the useful arts and protecting the property rights of authors. A more careful reading suggests that property rights were to be given to authors as a mechanism to promote the public good and not as an end in themselves (although the late eighteenth century marked the emergence of the author as a figure fully entitled to economic reward for their labor). Judicial interpretation and public understanding has tended to focus on the rights of authors to be rewarded for their labor. This focus became known as the labor or "sweat of the brow" theory of copyright. The legislature, oriented toward the present and future rather than precedent and compelled to review practices, may have been more mindful of the overall public good. Less noticed than the labor theory of copyright is the transformation of copyright in practice, at least in part, to a mechanism for projecting the labor of authors (or, with many forms of publication, the investment of publishers [P. Wilson, 1990]).

A potential conflict exists between public good and property rights in intellectual productions. Specifically, property rights can conflict with the freedom of expression guaranteed by the First Amendment to the U.S. Constitution. For example, the description or abstract of a document may approach the document described. It the document is factual, this gives property in facts, which would be a restraint on freedom of speech (P. Wilson, 1990).

The *Feist* judgment, concerned with intellectual property in telephone directories, acknowledges and reverses the labor theory of copyright:

> Article I, § 8, cl. 8, of the Constitution mandates originality as a prerequisite for copyright protection. The constitutional requirement necessitates independent creation plus a modicum of creativity. . . . The Copyright Act of 1976 and its predecessor, the Copyright Act of 1909, leave no doubt that originality is the touchstone of copyright protection in directories and other fact-based works. The 1976 Act explains that copyright extends to "original works of authorship," 17 U.S.C. § 102(a), and that there can be no copyright in facts, § 102(b). A compilation is not copyrightable *per se*, but is copyrightable only if its facts have been "selected, coordinated, or arranged in *such a way* that the resulting work as a whole constitutes an original work of authorship." § 101 (emphasis added). Thus, the statute envisions that some ways of selecting, coordinating, and arranging data are not sufficiently original to trigger copyright protection. Even a compilation that is copyrightable receives only limited protection, for the copyright does not extend to facts contained in the compilation. § 103(b). Lower courts that adopted a "sweat of the brow" or "industrious collection" test — which extended a compilation's copyright protection beyond selection and arrangement to the facts themselves — misconstrued the 1909 Act and eschewed the fundamental axiom of copyright law that no one may copyright facts or

> ideas. . . . Rural's selection of listings — subscribers' names, towns, and telephone numbers — could not be more obvious and lacks the modicum of creativity necessary to transform mere selection into copyrightable expression. In fact, it is plausible to conclude that Rural did not truly "select" to publish its subscribers' names and telephone numbers, since it was required to do so by state law. Moreover, there is nothing remotely creative about arranging names alphabetically in a white pages directory. It is an age-old practice, firmly rooted in tradition and so commonplace that it has come to be expected as a matter of course. . . . It may seem unfair that much of the fruit of the compiler's labor may be used by others without compensation. As Justice Brennan has correctly observed, however, this is not "some unforeseen byproduct of a statutory scheme." *Harper & Row,* 471 U.S., at 589 (dissenting opinion). It is, rather, "the essence of copyright," and a constitutional requirement. The primary objective of copyright is not to reward the labor of authors, but "to promote the Progress of Science and useful Arts." Art. I, § 8, cl. 8. *Accord Twentieth Century Music Corp. v. Aiken*, 422 U.S. 151, 156 (1975). To this end, copyright assures authors the right to their original expression, but encourages others to build freely upon the ideas and information conveyed by a work. (*Feist*, 1991)

The epistemology implied by the judgment conceives of facts existing independently of their discovery. The idea of selection, and of the degree of creativity in selection, also recurs. Most strikingly, the labor theory of copyright is reviewed, critiqued, and dismissed.

Why should this reversal have occurred at that time and place? The Supreme Court can override precedent and may resemble the legislature in its concern for public good and for interpreting the Constitution. The United States was being increasingly influenced by concepts of copyright held in other jurisdictions, marked by the, still minimalist, *Berne Convention Implementation Act* 1988 (although jurisdictions explicitly valuing dissemination above property rights, for instance the Soviet Union, would have been only indirectly influential) (see chapter 3). In terms of the dynamic developed here, the direct human labor involved in the selection, ordering, and presentation of data was no longer sufficiently substantial to warrant protection. The judgment regards this form of selection labor as "an age-old practice, firmly rooted in tradition and so commonplace that it has come to be expected as a matter of course." In practical terms, protecting public domain databases might have unacceptable costs.

A similar dynamic, principally the substitution of dead for living labor, has been detected in domains seldom viewed from a single perspective. The congruence in time, and, to some extent, in geopolitical region, between the development of the Internet and the departure from the labor theory of copyright is striking.

An information dynamic

Can an information dynamic then be constructed (see Figure 7.2)? Historically, human intellectual labor begins as semantic labor (natural signs could be regarded as analogous to objects of labor provided by nature) (Warner, 2001b). Over time, and through collective human endeavor, semantic labor can be transformed into syntactic labor, which can reduce the direct human intellectual labor required for semiotic processes. Particularly since the late nineteenth century, syntactic labor can be modeled and executed mechanically. In these processes of transformation, from spoken to written language, and, further, in computational modeling, a degree of exactness has to be imposed, which may reduce the vitality of the field. In the transformation to computable form, greater exactness is demanded (and this may expose as imperfect formalizations previously accepted as self-consistent). To interpret the results of these syntactic transformations, human semantic labor is required and the cycle is renewed.

Two distinct, but related, approaches could be taken to this dynamic.

- First, a priori to assert that universal (machine) labor cannot be semantic in character (following Searle, 1980).
- To accept this but then to suggest theoretical potentials and limitations on transformation of or modeling of semantic as syntactic labor.

The second approach promises to be more productive.

Some potentials and limitations can be suggested, connected with the self-identity of the sign and the limitations of exactness (or the exposure of the historical illusion of exactness).

- Heraclitus observed that no man stepped into the same river twice. In relation to the stream of oral speech, discussions have questioned the existence of synchronic synonymy. The diachronic analogue to synonymy, replication over time, has been

Figure 7.2. An information dynamic.

	Communal Labor		**Universal Labor**
Semantic	Natural signs (compare natural objects). Concept of number. Spoken language. Written language		
	Transition (Exactness)		
Syntactic	Grammar Logical and mathematical formalisms	**Transition (enhanced exactness)**	Mechanical modelling of logical and mathematical formalisms Syntactic transformations of written language Message transmission

discovered to be difficult to establish for oral forms, considered as signals, and, for the purposes of logical translation, for the signified for oral and written forms.

- The only identity required in formal logic is identity of the sign (Wittgenstein, 1981). It could be suggested that we can impose this convention of identity for certain purposes, within mathematics and logic, but not with fully publicly circulated messages. Once messages are fully in the public domain, their producers lose control over their transformation and interpretation.
- Loss of control may be a source of richness. From one semiotic perspective, all tautology (and, for Wittgenstein, logic consisted of tautologies) is a refusal of life.

Recognizing the potential and limitations of syntactic transformations may enhance our valuing of human intelligence and sympathies. Technology, regarded as a human construction, changes our conception of what it means to be human.

Conclusion

What is the value of this analysis? Previously unrelated developments can be viewed from a common perspective, enhancing our understanding of patterns. Particularly for information retrieval, research is brought simultaneously closer to ordinary discourse understandings, everyday practice, and to the human and social sciences.

The analysis may have predictive as well as analytic value, for instance for the proliferation of syntactically based information retrieval systems (although the predictive value of analyses of human domains is complicated by the effects of analyses on the consciousness and actions of human subjects and their activities).

Chapter 8

W(h)ither Information Science?

Suggestive, if not compelling, indications of a worldwide, or, more strictly, Anglo-American and English-language, crisis in library and information studies (LIS) can be found (Cronin, 1988; T.D. Wilson, 2000) (1; 2). A number of departments of LIS seem either to be retreating to, or inertly remaining, in established domains or being absorbed into other collectivities (e.g., management or communication studies) and losing their distinctive identity. Informal communication, particularly discussions with colleagues, would indicate that, to date, crises have been largely, although not entirely (Durrance and Pettigrew, 1999), perceived in local or intrainstitutional terms. The number of concurrent crises renders this perception unsatisfactory as a final explanation. It would be more convincing to regard them as products of a broader, quasi-global, movement mediated by local developments and conflicts. Perception in local terms may reflect imposition from outside the disciplinary community by educational funders and administrators, following a period of internal questioning in the late 1980s. Such a crisis demands explanation at a time when the information society concept, however diffusely understood, has captured the collective imagination (Webster, 1995a) and become a focus for research funding. The crisis also presents certain dangers and certain opportunities, particularly with the regard to the carrying forward of the intellectual inheritance of LIS. Although the primary focus here is upon LIS conceived, for analytical purposes, as a discipline partly autonomous from its base in professional practice, some reference will also be made to changes in the functions and roles of libraries and information professionals.

For an investigation of the issue, the premise must be accepted that the choice is not between a theoretically informed and a theoretically innocent account (understanding theory in its etymological sense of theater or situated viewpoint) but between theoretical awareness and unreflexive reproduction of implied ways of seeing. Information science has partly recognized, but not resolved, a problem of theoretical impoverishment and the limited recognition and resolution may themselves have contributed to the current crisis (Brown, 1987; Roberts, 1982; V. Rosenberg, 1974). The recurrent, even if only implied, antithesis between theory and practice is dissolved. It is accepted that practical understanding can be in advance of theoretical articulation, for instance, that the understanding embodied in the design and use of information retrieval systems may be in advance of classic information retrieval theory (see chapter 5).

Some analytical distinctions need to be introduced: between exoteric and esoteric communication, and between diachronic and synchronic perspectives. Exoteric would refer to the extracommunal or, in this instance, extradisciplinary sphere and esoteric to the intra-communal or intradisciplinary. The distinction has been developed for modeling the diffusion of specialized knowledge and can be applied at various levels of granularity (Warner, 1997). Diachronic is to be understood as the consideration of developments over time and synchronic as referring to a system or set of activities at a single point in time (Warner, 1994). Classically, from a linguistic perspective, the elements within a synchronic system exist in a network relation to one another, where changes in one item reverberate throughout the system, with particularly acute effects for neighboring elements (Saussure, 1983). These distinctions can help understand the coexistence of disciplines and tensions between diachronic inheritances and synchronic relations.

Historical Schema

A familiar analogy for the relation between disciplines is that of position in intellectual space (White and McCain, 1998). The concept of a discipline is recognized as problematic but is here regarded primarily as a group of people that may define itself in terms of subjects studied or methodologies favored. There may, and in the case of information studies will be, competition between different groups with common interests in subjects studied, but with contrasting historical antecedents (Ellis, Allen, and Wilson, T., 1999). The historical schema offered here is selective and provisional, although still, one hopes, illuminating (see Figure 8.1). The aim of the discursive commentary is not to repeat the diagrammatic presentation but to comment on its more significant aspects. In conformity with established conventions, synchronic relations are read across the table and diachronic inheritances downwards. Exoteric (to LIS) and esoteric (within LIS) developments are distinguished and information science differentiated from library studies.

The review can begin, in order to simplify issues, in the post-1945 period, although significant antecedents are not forgotten. Information science and library studies can, for the immediate post-1945 period, in a further simplification, be regarded as largely separate developments with contrasting intellectual antecedents and with different responses to information technologies. Information science has been regarded as a response to developments in telecommunications and computer technology, during that period (Brown, 1987; see chapter 2). Although the formal development of information science is often traced to the mid-1950s and to the concern to prevent diseconomies in the discovery of scientific information (the development of Sputnik is cited as a particular stimulus), people in information science tended to seek explanatory models and to derive techniques from information theory, particularly Claude Shannon's seminal work (Lynch, 1977; Shannon and Weaver, 1949), from emergent computer science, and from cybernetics. These influences, particularly Shannon's information theory, still persist, albeit in qualified and modified form (Cole, 1999). More broadly, information scientists of the period were influenced by notions of rationality and experimental method. These ways of thinking reveal themselves in the information retrieval experiments initiated, partly independently, in Britain and North America in the late 1950s (Ellis, 1992). Their persistence, demonstrated, for instance, in the continuity from the Cranfield experiments to the Text Retrieval Experimental Conference (TREC), testifies to the power of those ways of thought and to the institutional embedding of experimental information retrieval, despite compelling critiques and limited influence on practice (Ellis, 1984).

For library studies, Shera and Egan's proposal for social epistemology, the study of social not primarily individual ways of knowing, with the intention of informing bibliographic arrangements, was made but has only been partly continued (Shera, 1965a). Currently available full-text data gives a historically unparalleled resource for tracing the diffusion of ideas. Social epistemology could be revived within information science, partly conceived as an end in itself (Warner, 1997) (3). Humanistic resistance to modern information technology was still powerful in the post-1945 period. An "acculturation of the machine" was conceived as one aspect of social epistemology, but this has only been pursued by some rather isolated contributions (Shera, 1965b; Warner, 1993a). Public and humanistic resistance to new technologies has declined, but more through a process of diffusion of technologies, including both their naturalization and transformation into more immediately useable resources (Warner, 1991; see chapter 2).

The 1960s and 1970s witnessed the study of information science and librarianship within single institutional collectivities, although still partly showing contrasting intellectual antecedents. In the early and mid-1970s, proposals for a social science approach to information science were developed. Some of these would now be read primarily as historical documents (Roberts, 1976) while others, for instance, those concerned with the complexity of relevance (P. Wilson, 1973) and indexing for the social sciences (Watson and others, 1973), have continuing relevance, evidenced by their occasional citation. Librarianship and information science also began to be studied in a more integrated fashion, with one understanding developed that information science was to be differentiated from librarianship by its active intervention in the process of communication (Roberts, 1977). The social science approach to library and information studies was carried forward in certain institutional contexts. Other information scientists, in greater number, continued with experimental information retrieval in the Cranfield tradition and to seek models and techniques from information theory. Simultaneously, and powerfully, emerging in the exoteric realm, specifically within the social sciences, was the concept of the post-industrial or information society (D. Bell, 1980). The impression of LIS in this period is of valuable, although numerically relatively limited, intellectual developments and of continuity from the immediate post-1945 period, but not of comparable intellectual vitality and innovation.

Two crucial diffusion processes occurred during the 1980s: the further diffusion, and developing critiques, of the information society concept; and the spread of computer, particularly microcomputer, technology. Possibly consequentially, humanistic resistance to modern information technologies began to erode. From a network conception of the synchronic coexistence of disciplines, two associated developments can be recognized: within LIS, the diffusion of computer technologies in use, although not necessarily in design and construction, was associated with reduced differences between librarianship and information science; and the exoteric diffusion of information concepts and technologies assisted the development of groups likely to occupy subject domains similar to or contiguous with LIS, acting, in effect, as competitors. Conversely, the exoteric growth of information concepts also represented an opportunity to expand the scope and wider contribution of LIS. A critical period for expansion may have occurred in the early 1980s. The growth of exoteric competitors may make it difficult to revive this opportunity. In the mid to late 1980s, LIS began intensive questioning of its research and educational mission, with some formal reviews conducted (Davinson and Roberts, 1986; Transbinary Group, 1986; Wood, 1992).

The 1990s saw the continued diffusion of information society concepts and of computer technologies, with associated developments in the configuration of disciplines. The information society debate was more strongly carried by disciplines in the exoteric sphere, such as sociology (Webster, 1995a), with LIS losing, or not acquiring, substantial public conviction as a contributor to the discussion; and scholarly interests in information retrieval continued to be developed in computer science. Bibliographic retrieval, including scientific and chemical information, remained a continuing component of LIS. With increasing ease of use of such retrieval systems, the location of LIS professional expertise may have shifted from understanding how to use systems to selection amongst them. Similarly, libraries persisted as institutions and as educational foci. The crucial dangers are of intellectual isolation and the associated double penalty: a reduction in the richness of LIS; and a failure to contribute from LIS to the exoteric sphere. From the early 1990s, crises in LIS education and research begin to develop (Ostler, Dahlin, and Willardson, 1995; Stieg, 1992; P. Wilson, 1993; 1996b).

Analogous developments are occurring with regard to the configuration of the professional societies in the LIS field and significant aspects of professional practice. The Institute of Information Scientists (IIS) (covering the United Kingdom and the Republic of Ireland) is poised between union with, or assimilation to, the Library Association and the construction of broader alliances, for instance, with the British Computer Society. The numerical predominance of the membership is strongly towards union with the Library Association. The IIS has also been marked by a concern with boundary and field definition, unconsciously revealing a characteristic of a declining organization — emerging movements may be content with unexplicated manifestos ("We hold these truths to be self-evident."). The American Society for Information Science has, more recently, realized the vulnerability created by its declining membership (4). Information and library science functions, such as document delivery, information system design, and acting as information intermediaries have also diffused widely beyond the established information professions, although libraries as physical institutions persist. A recent review notes this development and characterizes the claim that "access to graphic records, in whatever form, is under the control of the librarian" as "preposterous": "Were that so, librarians would have good reason to think very well of themselves. But tell it to any bookseller or any kid surfing the Net. . . . (the author) is surely right . . . that the need for intermediaries, guides, advisers, and helpers in finding useful information will not disappear. Quite the contrary, but he has no arguments for expecting that librarians will play a prominent, much less a dominant, part in the business of intermediation" (P. Wilson, 2000, 137).

The analogy adopted here of intellectual space for the configuration of disciplines would be misleading, if attention were not also paid to their conditions for production and renewal. Disciplines do not float in intellectual space any more than a language exists independently of its producers (Vološinov, 1986). With the professionalization of certain forms of intellectual labor, disciplines are produced and renewed on the basis of public and private subsidies generated from labor in the exoteric realm. A further consideration would be the mass of a discipline and its persuasive political resource for self-renewal. Disciplines are carried forward by institutions and by individuals working in institutional contexts: there can be extensive patterns of personal transmission and inheritance, particularly with regard to research supervisors or advisors influencing the destination of and possibilities for graduate students (these are observable in classic information retrieval research). Under relatively stable contexts or conditions, where, for instance, the subjects of study are relatively coterminous with the discipline's interests, there are mechanisms that serve to forget, carry forward, renew, and, if necessary, rediscover intellectual contributions.

The current situation in LIS can, then, be regarded as indicative of a crisis exoterically imposed by educational funders and administrators not convinced of the discipline's value (Stieg, 1992; P. Wilson, 2000). The scholarly community may also be below critical mass for ensuring its renewal through political persuasion, although there are geopolitical contrasts, for instance, between the United States and the United Kingdom. From a Kuhnian perspective, scholarly communities tend to change radically or die, not from internal changes in conviction but from a failure to attract sufficient talented recruits, and there are anecdotal and published (Browne, 1999) accounts of difficulties, at various levels, in recruitment. There is a danger that what is valuable in LIS will be forgotten or revert to a relatively enclosed niche, unless deliberate strategies are developed to prevent reversion. Insights developed in LIS may then be painfully, and uneconomically, recreated at a later date and there are already cases of this and realizations of the need for continuity from LIS (Griffiths, 2000; Hjørland, 2000) — "if Ranganathan were alive today he would be aware of the potential of his ideas for searching and organising WWW materials" (Ellis and Vasconceloss, 1999). Independent recreation would run counter to a classic rationale for information science, to prevent diseconomies in research.

A strong degree of responsibility must be attached to information science itself for failing to command exoteric conviction, particularly with regard to the limited resolution of its theoretical impoverishment. The impression, although not the exclusive impression, is of a rather weary, but still continuing, empiricism. For instance, in the absence of a shaping conception of "information man," user studies produced a catalog of particularities of limited use in system design (Roberts, 1982). More recently, a treatment within LIS of the information society was regarded as having imported this crucial concept largely as a label, without fuller conceptual awareness: "theoretically and conceptually naïve and uninformed . . . does not appear to be bothered to encounter the major contributions of other scholars . . . This is not to ask for esoteric and recondite theorization, just for some familiarization with the major contributions of Daniel Bell, Herbert Schiller, James Beniger and such thinkers . . . flawed by intellectual laziness" (Webster, 1995b, 175). The primarily exoteric reviewer was writing in an esoteric (LIS) context and does acknowledge the work's local clarity. The second edition of the work reveals no response to this devastating critique. Curiously, the comment on its clarity is quoted on the cover (5) (Feather, 1994; 1998). The indifference implied to the critique is a disturbing, if minor, sign of the limited awareness of the significance of the issues raised.

Some more hopeful developments are also occurring. Library history is being revived by a reintegration into its wider intellectual context (Black, 1998). McKenzie's proposal for "sociology of texts" (McKenzie, 1986), not necessarily sympathetically received within bibliography, has been advocated as a basis for an expansive information studies (P. Wilson, 1996c). Such developments recognize the significance of the exoteric intellectual context, although do not address exoteric communities directly. Other developments, for instance computer science as a human science (Sawyer Seminar, 2000) and, in particular, social informatics combine esoteric (LIS) and exoteric affiliations. It might be these latter developments that will carry forward and disseminate what is valuable in LIS.

Conclusion

The forces identified here as making for a quasi-global crisis in LIS, the diffusion of modern information technologies in use and the spread of the scholarly interest in information, are unlikely to diminish. The historical forces that produced modern information technologies and information science (Brown, 1987; see chapter 2) may now dissolve it, or, given strategic action, enable it to expand and develop. The tension between the diachronic inheritance of information science and its synchronic circumstances would seem to enforce a choice between reversion to niches, either deliberate or apathetic, with its attendant danger of intellectual isolation, or participation in wider information collectivities. The binary choice presented has implications for academic administrative as well as intellectual boundaries. The rhetoric of the presentation here should have made the preference for wider participation clear: the challenge posed to information science in 1987, "to broaden its academic remit to include serious consideration of the 'information society' and how it interlocks with the total social situation" (Brown, 1987, 113), remains relevant. In addressing it, information science might be enabled to become an exporter as well as an importer of ideas, its more customary role (Cronin and Pearson, 1990). The issue confronting information science could be regarded as a particular case of what any intellectual accumulation poses, how, as Caxton requested, to: "take the good and honest actes in their remembraunce, and to folowe the same . . . Doo after the good and leve the evyl, and it shal brynge you to good fame and renommee" (Caxton, 1978, xv).

There are the hopeful developments of computer science as a human science and of social informatics, and, from personal observation, of students from the social sciences and humanities entering information science, resistant to approaches dominated by logical formulations and scientific expectations, but not yet able fully to articulate a counter dialogue. This potential may develop. The value of the account and analysis presented here would be to inform strategies for such developments.

Figure 8.1. Diachronic and synchronic perspectives on LIS.

Date			1945-
Exoteric developments			
	Information science	Theoretical precursors / inherited ways of thinking in logic, mathematics, and engineering	Cybernetics, information theory (associating information and uncertainty); computer science (emergent)
Esoteric developments			
	Librarian-ship	Library studies	

Figure 8.1. Diachronic and synchronic perspectives on LIS.

1950s	1960s	1970s
		Emergence of postindustrial or information society concept (from social sciences and sociology)
Scientific, including chemical, information		Social science approach to information science carried forward in certain institutional contexts
Intellectual backgrounds of information scientists (notions of rationality and experimental method: consider information retrieval experiments)	Librarianship and information science studied within single institutional collectivities (but with contrasting intellectual antecedents)	Proposals for a social science approach to information since and unified consideration of information and library science
Influence of Shera and Egan: social epistemology		
Humanistic resistance to technology	Social epistemology not fully continued	

Figure 8.1. Diachronic and synchronic perspectives on LIS.

1980s	
Diffusion (and critiques) of information society concept; Information society concept carried forward more by sociology than information science	
Diffusion of computer technologies in use	Development of computer technologies carried forward more (not exclusively) by computer science than information and library science
Internal questioning of educational and research mission	
Diffusion of computer technologies in use	Reduction in humanistic resistance to technologies

Figure 8.1. Diachronic and synchronic perspectives on LIS.

	1990s	
Questioning by funders of LIS	TREC continues experimental information retrieval (with some modifications to improve robustness of methodology)	
	TREC also includes some contributors from information science	Information science as a social science carried (possibly) by social informatics and computer science as a human science
Crises perceived in local terms by participants, but number of simultaneous events	Continued interest in scientific and chemical information (although ease of use of systems has enforced relocation of professional expertise)	
	Loss/not acquisition of conviction in information society debate (intellectual insurality)	Social epistemology partly carried forward by philosophy and other disciplinary interests
	Continuity of libraries as institutions and educational foci (danger of intellectual isolation)	

Notes

1. Forms of educational and library organization in other geopolitical regions, for instance, Mediterranean Europe and the former Soviet Union, have been different.

2. There are geopolitical contrasts within the Anglo-American and English-language regions and the crisis also offers opportunities. The absence of a comprehensive account of the current situation suggests a theoretical paucity rather than a theoretical conflict within LIS.

3. The journal *Social Epistemology* emerges primarily from an independent sociological tradition and is not concerned with informing bibliographic arrangements.

4. These observations are informed by participation in discussions at IIS National Council (1994-1999) and ASIS Annual Meetings (1996-1999). The IIS merged with the Library Association to form the Chartered Institute of Library and Information Professionals (CILIP), with the new body formally brought into existence in 2002. ASIS became the American Society for Information Science and Technology (ASIS&T) in 2000 and expanded its interests.

5. A more charitable age might have allowed full obscurity to these errors of omission, *pace* Samuel Johnson: "To illustrate this remark, by the mention of obscure names, would not much confirm it" (Johnson, 1984, 118); but modern editorial practice requires specific citations.

Bibliography

Abrams, H. B. (1991). *The Law of Copyright*. New York: Clark Boardman Company.

Attali, J., and Y. Stourdze (1977). The birth of the telephone and economic crisis: the slow death of monologue in French society. In I. de Sola Pool (Ed.). *The Social Impact of the Telephone* (pp. 97-111). Cambridge, Mass.: MIT Press.

Aune, D. E. (1987). Oracles. In E. Mircea (Ed.). *The Encyclopaedia of Religion* (volume 2, pp. 80-87). New York: Macmillan.

Bacon, F. (1973). *The Advancement of Learning*. Edited by G. W. Kitchin. Introduction by Arthur Johnston. London: Dent.

———. (1985). Of studies. In F. Bacon. *The Essays*. Edited with an introduction by John Pitcher. Harmondsworth, England: Penguin Books.

Bar-Hillel, Y. (1964). An examination of information theory. In Y. Bar-Hillel. *Language and Information: Selected Essays on Their Theory and Application*. Reading, Mass.: Addison-Wesley.

Belkin. N. J., and A. Vickery (1985). *Interaction in Information Systems: A Review of Research from Document Retrieval to Knowledge-Based Systems*. (Library and Information Research Report 35). London: British Library.

Belkin, N. J., and W. B. Croft (1987) "Retrieval techniques." *Annual Review of Information Science and Technology*, 22, 109-145.

Bell, A. (1980). *Sydney Smith*. Oxford: Clarendon Press.

Bell, D. (1980). The social framework of the information society. In T. Forester (Ed.). *The Microelectronics Revolution: The Complete Guide to the New Technology and Its Impact on Society* (pp. 500-549). Oxford: Basil Blackwell.

Beniger, J. R. (1986). *The Control Revolution: Technological and Economic Origins of the Information Society*. Cambridge, Mass.: Harvard University Press.

Berne Convention (1886). *Berne Convention of September 9th, 1886*. In F. E. Skone James. *Copinger on the Law of Copyright* (pp. 397-422). 6th edition. London: Sweet and Maxwell, 1927.

Biber, D. (1988). *Variation across Speech and Writing*. Cambridge, England: Cambridge University Press.

Bishop, W. P. (1959). The struggle for international copyright in the United States. Ph.D. dissertation, Boston University.

Black, A. (1998). "Information and modernity: the history of information and the eclipse of library history." *Library History*. 14, 39-45.

Blair, D., and W. Maron (1990). "Full-text information retrieval: further analysis and clarification." *Information Processing & Management*, 26, 437-47.

Bochenski, I. M. (1961). *History of Formal Logic*. Translated by I. Thomas. Notre Dame, Ind.: University of Notre Dame Press.

Boosey, W. (1931). *Fifty Years of Music*. London: Ernest Benn.

Boosey v. White. (1899). *Boosey v. White*. Appeal from the Chancery division. Dec. 4, 5, and 13, 1899. (Before Lindley, M. R., Sir Francis Jeune, and L. J. Romer). *The Law Times Reports*, 81, 571-75.

Boucicault v. Wood. (1867). *Boucicault v. Wood*. (Circuit Court, N. D. Illinois – November term 1867). 3F. Cas 9888 (No. 1693) 2 Biss. 34. In *Decisions of the United States Courts Involving Copyright and Literary Property* (Copyright Office Bulletin) (vol. 13, pp. 411-16). Washington, D.C.: Copyright Office, Library of Congress, 1909.

Bradford, S. C. (1971). *Documentation*. London: C. Lockwood.

Braunstein, Y. M. (1987). "Economics of intellectual property rights in the international arena." *Journal of the American Society for Information Science*. 40, 12-16.

Brown, A. D. (1987). *Towards a Theoretical Information Science: Information Science and the Concept of a Paradigm* (University of Sheffield Department of Information Studies, Occasional Publications Series, No. 5). Sheffield: University of Sheffield, Department of Information Studies.

Browne, M. (1999). "Threat or Promise? The Information Society and The Information Profession." *Australian Library Journal*. 48, 17-32.

Bryson, B. (1998). *Made in America*. London: Black Swan.

Buckland, M. (1991). "Information as thing." *Journal of the American Society for Information Science*. 42, 351-60.

———. (1999). "The landscape of information science: the American Society for Information Science at 62." *Journal of the American Society for Information Science*. 50, 970-74.

Buckland, M., and C. Plaunt (1994). "On the construction of selection systems." *Library Hi Tech*. 12, 15-28.

Buhle, P. (1991). *Marxism in the United States: Remapping the History of the American Left*. 2nd rev. edition. London: Verso.

Carlyle, T. (1971). Chartism. In T. Carlyle. *Selected Writings*. Edited by A. Shelston (pp. 149-232). London: Penguin.

Caxton, W. (1978). Caxton's Preface. In T. Malory. *Works*. Edited by E. Vinaver (pp. xiii-xv). Oxford: Oxford University Press.

Cayton, M. K. (1993). Print and publishing. In M. K. Cayton, E. J. Gorn, and P. W. Williams (Eds.). *Encyclopedia of American Social History* (pp. 2427-445). New York: Charles Scribner's Sons.

Cayton, M. K., Gorn, E. J. and Williams, P. W. (Eds.) (1993). *Encyclopedia of American Social History*. New York: Charles Scribner's Sons.

Cayton, R. L. (1993). The early national period. In M. K. Cayton, E. J. Gorn, P. W. Williams (Eds.). *Encyclopedia of American Social History* (pp. 87-104). New York: Charles Scribner's Sons.

Chesterton, G. K. (1925). *Charles Dickens*. 15th edition. London: Methuen & Co., Ltd.

Clark, A. J. (1960). *The Movement for International Copyright in Nineteenth Century America*. Washington, D.C.: Catholic University of America.

Cole, C. (1999). "Activity of understanding a problem during interaction with an 'enabling' information retrieval system: modeling information flow." *Journal of the American Society for Information Science*. 50, 544-52.

Collins, R. (1979). *The Credentials Society: A Historical Sociology of Education and Stratification*. New York: Academic Press.

———. (1998). *The Sociology of Philosophies: A Global Theory of Intellectual Change*. Cambridge, Mass.: The Belknap Press of Harvard University Press.

Constitution (1789). The Constitutional provision concerning copyright. In M. B. Nimmer. *Nimmer On Copyright: A Treatise on the Law of Literary, Musical and Artistic Property, and the Protection of Ideas* (appendix 1). Albany, N.Y.: M. Bender, 1963-1991.

Copyright Act (1790). *An Act for the Encouragement of Learning by Securing the Copies of Maps, Charts, and Books, to the Authors and Proprietors of Such Copies, During the Time therein Mentioned*. May 31, 1790. First Congress. Sess. II. Ch. 15.

Copyright Act (1802). *An Act Supplementary to an Act, Intituled "An Act for the Encouragement of Learning by Securing the Copies of Maps, Charts, and Books, to the Authors and Proprietors of Such Copies, During the Time therein Mentioned." and Extending the Benefits Thereof to the Arts of Designing, Engraving, and Etching*

Historical and Other Prints. April 29, 1802. Seventh Congress. Sess. I. Ch. 36.

Copyright Act (1831). *An Act to Amend the Several Acts Respecting Copyrights*. February 3, 1831. Twenty-First Congress. Sess. II. Ch. 16.

Copyright Act. (1842). *An Act to Amend the Law of Copyright*. 1842. 5 and 6 Victoria ch.xlv.3.

Copyright Act (1865). *An Act Supplemental to an Act Entitled "An Act to Amend the Several Acts Respecting Copyright,"* Approved February Third, Eighteen Hundred and Thirty-one, and to the Acts in Addition thereto and Amendment thereof. March 3, 1865. Thirty-Eighth Congress. Sess. II. Ch. 126.

Copyright Act (1867). *An Act Amendatory of the Several Acts Respecting Copyrights*. February 13, 1867. Thirty-Ninth Congress. Sess. II. Ch. 43.

Copyright Act (1870). *An Act to Revise, Consolidate, and Amend the Statutes Relating to Patents and Copyrights*. July 8, 1870. Forty-First Congress. Sess. II. Ch. 230.

Copyright Act (1882). *An Act to Amend the Statutes in Relation to Copyright*. August 1, 1882. Forty-Seventh Congress. Session I. Ch. 366.

Copyright Act (1891). *An Act to Amend Title Sixty, Chapter Three, of the Revised Statutes of the United States, relating to Copyrights*. March 3, 1891. Fifty-First Congress. Sess. II. Ch. 565.

Copyright Act (1911) *Copyright Act 1911*. 1 and 2 George V. ch. 46.

Copyright Decisions (1909). *Decisions of the United States Courts Involving Copyright and Literary Property 1789-1909*. Washington, D.C.: Copyright Office, Library of Congress.

Cronin, B. (1998). Library and information science in context. In M. Line, G. Mackenzie, and P. Sturges (Eds.). *Librarianship and Information Work Worldwide* (pp. 1-17). London: Bowker-Saur.

Cronin, B., and E. Davenport (2001). "E-Rogeneous zones: positioning pornography in the digital economy." *The Information Society*. 17, 33-48.

Cronin, B., and S. Pearson (1990). "The export of ideas from information science." *Journal of Information Science*. 16, 381-91.

Darwin, C. (1968) *The Origin of Species by Means of Natural Selection Or The Preservation of Favoured Races in the Struggle For Life*. Edited by J. W. Burrow. London: Penguin Group.

Davinson, D., and N. Roberts (1986). "Developments in information education and their implications for schools of librarianship and information studies in the United Kingdom." *Journal of Documentation*, 42, 1-10.

Dempsey, L., and R. Heery (1998). "Metadata: A current view of practice and issues." *Journal of Documentation*, 54, 145-72.

Dickens, C. (1946). *Great Expectations*. London: Oxford University Press.

———. (1982). *American Notes for General Circulation*. Harmondsworth, England: Penguin Books.

———. (1989). *Hard Times*. Edited with an introduction and notes by Paul Schlicke. Oxford: Oxford University Press.

Dijkstra, E. W. (1989). "On the cruelty of really teaching computer science (The SIGCSE Award Lecture 1989)." *SIGCSE Bulletin: a Quarterly Publication of the Special Interest Group on Computer Science Education*, 21, xxiv-xxxix.

Durrance, J. C., and K. E. Pettigrew (1999). Kaliper: a look at library and information science education at the turn of a new century. In *Bowker Annual Library and Book Trade Almanac*. Edited by Bowker staff (pp. 266-281). New Providence, N.J.: Bowker.

Easterlin, R. A. (1980). Population. In G. Porter (Ed.). *Encyclopedia of American Economic History* (volume 1, pp. 167-82). New York: Charles Scribner's Sons.

Economist. (1996). "Retribution for reproduction." *Economist*. 18 May 1996, 73-74.

Ellis, D. (1984). "Theory and explanation in information retrieval research." *Journal of Information Science*. 8, 25-38.

———. (1990). *New Horizons in Information Retrieval*. London: Library Association.

———. (1992). "The physical and cognitive paradigms in information retrieval research." *Journal of Documentation*. 48, 45-64.

———. (1996). *Progress and Problems in Information Retrieval*. London: Library Association.

Ellis, D., D. Allen, and T. Wilson (1999). "Information science and information systems: conjunct subjects disjunct disciplines." *Journal of the American Society for Information Science*. 50, 1095-107.

Ellis, D., and A. Vasconceloss (1999). "Ranganathan and the Net: using facet analysis to search and organize the World Wide Web." *Aslib Proceedings*. 51, 3-10.

Encyclopaedia Britannica. (1911). Copyright. In *The Encyclopaedia Britannica*. 11th edition (volume 8, pp. 118-129). Cambridge, England: Cambridge University Press.

Feather, J. (1994). *The Information Society: A Study of Continuity and Change*. London: Library Association Publishing.

———. (1998). *The Information Society: A Study of Continuity and Change*. 2nd edition. London: Library Association Publishing.

Feist (1991). *Feist Publications, Inc., v. Rural Telephone Service Co., Inc.* No. 89-1909. Supreme Court of the United States. January 9, 1991, argued. March 27, 1991, decided.

Finnegan, R. (1989). "Communication and technology." *Language and Communication: An Interdisciplinary Journal*. 9, 107-27.

Forster, J. (1928). *The Life of Charles Dickens*. Edited by J. W. T. Ley. London: Cecil Palmer.

Freeman, C. (1987). Innovation. In J. Eatwell, M. Milgate, and P. Newman (Eds). *The New Palgrave: A Dictionary of Economics* (volume 2, 858-860). 4 volumes. London: Macmillan.

Gardin, J-C. (1973). "Document analysis and linguistic theory." *Journal of Documentation*. 29, 137-68.

Gardner, M. (1958). *Logic Machines and Diagrams*. Brighton, England: Harvester.

Gilfillan, S. C. (1970). *The Sociology of Invention*. Cambridge, Mass.: MIT Press.

Gilmore-Lehne, W. J. (1993). Literacy. In M. K. Cayton, E. J. Gorn, and P. W. Williams (Eds.). *Encyclopedia of American Social History* (pp. 2413-426). New York: Charles Scribner's Sons.

Goodrum, C. A. (1986). National libraries. In R. Wedgeworth (Ed.). *ALA World Encyclopedia of Library and Information Services* (pp. 830-838). 2nd edition. Chicago: American Library Association.

Goody, J., and I. Watt (1968). The consequences of literacy. In J. Goody (Ed.). *Literacy in Traditional Societies*. Cambridge, England: Cambridge University Press.

Graham, G. (1999). *The Internet: A Philosophical Enquiry*. London: Routledge.

Griffiths, J. M. (2000). "Back to the future: Information science for the new millennium." *Bulletin of the American Society for Information Science*. 26, 24-27.

Gringal'ts, I. A. (1973). Copyright. In *Great Soviet Encyclopedia* (A translation of the 3rd edition) (volume 1, pp. 597-598). New York: Macmillan.

Grossman, J. R. (1994a). Introduction. In J. R. Grossman (Ed.). *The Frontier in American Culture* (An exhibition at the Newberry Library, August 26, 1994 – January 7, 1995) (pp. 1-5). Los Angeles, Calif.: University of California Press.

Grossman, J. R. (Ed.) (1994b). *The Frontier in American Culture* (An exhibition at the Newberry Library, August 26, 1994 – January 7, 1995). Los Angeles, Calif.: University of California Press.

Hancock-Beaulieu, M. (Ed.) (1992). *Information Systems for End-Users: Research and Development Issues*. London: Taylor Graham.

Harris, R. (1986). *The Origin of Writing*. London: Duckworth.

———. (1989) "How does writing restructure thought?" *Language & Communication*. 9, 99-106.

Harter, S. P., and C. A. Hert (1997). "Evaluation of information retrieval systems: approaches, issues, and methods." *Annual Review of Information Science and Technology*. 32, 3-94.

Haye, Y. de la (Ed.) (1980). *Marx & Engels on the Means of Communication (The Movement of Commodities, People, Information & Capital): A Selection of Texts*. New York: International General.

Heine, M. H. (1980). "The "question" as a fundamental variable in information science." In O. Harbo and L. Kajberg (Eds.). *Theory and Application of Information Research* (Proceedings of the Second International Research Forum on Information Science, 3-6 August 1977, Royal School of Librarianship, Copenhagen) (pp. 137-145). London: Mansell.

———. (1983). "Review of R. N. Oddy, S. E. Robertson, C. J. van Rijsbergen and P. W. Williams (Eds.). *Information Retrieval Research*." *Social Science Information Studies*. 3, 59-60.

Hjørland, B. (2000). "Library and information science: practice, theory, and philosophical basis." *Information Processing & Management*, 36, 501-31.

Holland, M. J. (1978). A brief history of American copyright law. In Herbert S. White (Ed.). *The Copyright Dilemma* (Proceedings of a conference held at Indiana University April 14-15, 1977) (pp. 3-26). Chicago: American Library Association.

Howells, R. (1999). "A movie murder mystery." *The Times Higher Education Supplement*. 23 July 1999, 18-19.

John, R. R. (1993). Communications and information processing. In M. K. Cayton, E. J. Gorn, and P. W. Williams (Eds.). *Encyclopedia of American Social History* (pp. 2349-361). New York: Charles Scribner's Sons.

Johnson, S. (1984). An Account of the Harleian Library. In D. Greene (Ed.). *Samuel Johnson* (pp. 117-119). Oxford: Oxford University Press.

Kahin, B., and C. Nesson (Eds.). (1997). *Borders in Cyberspace: Information Policy and the Global Information Infrastructure*. Cambridge, Mass.: MIT Press.

Kling, R., H. Rosenbaum, and C. Hert. (1998). "Social informatics in information science: an introduction." *Journal of the American Society for Information Science*. 49, 1047-52.

Kling, R., and G. McKim, G. (1999). "Scholarly communication and the continuum of electronic publishing." *Journal of the American Society for Information Science*. 50, 890-906.

Kneale, W. K., and M. Kneale (1962). *The Development of Logic*. Oxford: Clarendon Press.

Kuhn, T. S. (1970). *The Structure of Scientific Revolutions*. 2nd edition. Chicago: University of Chicago Press.

Leith, P. (1990). *Formalism in AI and Computer Science*. New York: Ellis Horwood.

Levinson, P. (1997). *The Soft Edge: A Natural History and Future of the Information Revolution*. London: Routledge.

Limerick, P. N. (1994). Travels in frontierland. In J. R. Grossman (Ed.). *The Frontier in American Culture*. An exhibition at the Newberry Library, August 26, 1994 – January 7, 1995 (pp. 67-102). Los Angeles, Calif.: University of California Press.

Lukács, G. (1973). Technology and social relations. In G. Lukács, *Marxism and Human Liberation: Essays On History, Culture and Revolution*. Edited with an introduction by E. San Juan Jr. (pp. 49-60). New York: Delta.

Lynch, M. F. (1977). "Variety generation – a reinterpretation of Shannon's Mathematical Theory of Communication, and its implications for information science." *Journal of the American Society for Information Science*. 28, 19-25.

Lyotard, J-F. (1979). *The Postmodern Condition: A Report on Knowledge*. Translated by G. Bennington and B. Massumi. Minneapolis, Minn.: University of Minnesota Press.

Mackenzie, D. (1996). *Knowing Machines: Essays on Technical Change*. Cambridge, Mass.: MIT Press.

Madison, J. H. (1980). Communications. In G. Porter (Ed.). *Encyclopedia of American Economic History* (volume 1, pp. 335-43). New York: Charles Scribner's Sons.

Mandel, E. (1976). Introduction. In K. Marx. *Capital: A Critique of Political Economy*. Volume 1. Introduced by Ernest Mandel. Translated by Ben Fowkes. Harmondsworth, England: Penguin Books in association with New Left Review.

Martin, A. (1980). Economy from reconstruction to 1914. In G. Porter (Ed.). *Encyclopedia of American Economic History* (volume 1, pp. 91-109). New York: Charles Scribner's Sons.

Marx, K. (1973a). *Grundrisse: Foundations of the Critique of Political Economy (Rough Draft)*. Translated with a foreword by Martin Nicolaus. London: Penguin Books in association with New Left Review.

———. (1973b). *The Eighteenth Brumaire of Louis Bonaparte*. In K. Mark, *Surveys from Exile: Political Writings*. Edited by David Fernbach (volume 2, 143-249). Harmondsworth, England: Penguin Books in association with New Left Review.

———. (1975). Preface to *A Contribution to The Critique of Political Economy*. In K. Marx, *Early Writings*. Introduced by Lucio Colletti. Translated by Rodney Livingstone and Gregor Benton. Harmondsworth, England: Penguin Books in association with New Left Review.

———. (1976). *Capital: A Critique of Political Economy*. Volume 1. Introduced by Ernest Mandel. Translated by Ben Fowkes. Harmondsworth, England: Penguin Books in association with New Left Review.

———. (1981). *Capital: A Critique of Political Economy*. Volume Three. Introduced by Ernest Mandel. Translated by David Fernbach. Harmondsworth, England: Penguin Books in association with New Left Review.

Marx, K., and F. Engels (1998). *The Communist Manifesto: A Modern Edition*. With an introduction by E. Hobsbawm. London: Verso.

Mattelart, A. (1996). *The Invention of Communication*. Translated by Susan Emanuel. Minneapolis: University of Minnesota Press.

McCarthy, J. T. (1991). *McCarthy's Desk Encyclopedia of Intellectual Property*. Washington, D.C.: Bureau of National Affairs.

McClelland, P. D. (1980). Transportation. In G. Porter (Ed.). *Encyclopedia of American Economic History* (volume 1, pp. 309-34). New York: Charles Scribner's Sons, 1980.

McGee, V. (1998). Semantic paradoxes and the theory of truth. In E. Craig (Ed.). *Routledge Encyclopedia of Philosophy* (volume 8, pp. 642-48). London: Routledge.

McKenzie, D. F. (1986). *Bibliography and the Sociology of Texts* (The Panizzi Lectures, 1985). London: British Library.

Minsky, M. (1967). *Computation: Finite and Infinite Machines*. Englewood Cliffs, N.J.: Prentice-Hall.

Moore, G. H. (1998). Logic in the early 20th century. In E. Craig (Ed.). *Routledge Encyclopedia of Philosophy* (Volume 5, pp. 729-38). London: Routledge.

Mowery, D. C., and N. Rosenberg, N. (1998). *Paths of Innovation: Technological Change in 20th Century America*. Cambridge, England: Cambridge University Press.

Nelson, R. R. (1969). Innovation. In D. L. Sills (Ed.). *International Encyclopedia of the Social Sciences* (volume 7, 339-45). New York: Macmillan.

Nimmer, D. (1986). Copyright. In K. L. Karst, D. J. Mahoney (Eds.). *Encyclopedia of the American Constitution* (pp. 504-5). New York: Macmillan.

———. (1990). *Nimmer On Copyright: Computer Law, Software Protection, Intellectual Property Counseling & Litigation, and Entertainment Industry Contracts; The Berne Convention Implementation Act of 1988*. New York: M. Bender.

Numbers, R. L. (1993). Science as a profession. In M. K. Cayton, E. J. Gorn, and P. W. Williams (Eds.). *Encyclopedia of American Social History* (pp. 2285-95). New York: Charles Scribner's Sons.

Ohlman, H. (1996). Information: timekeeping, computing, telecommunications and audiovisual technologies. In Ian McNeil (Ed.). *An Encyclopaedia of the History of Technology* (pp. 686-758). London: Routledge.

Ollé, J. G. (1986). Panizzi. In R. Wedgeworth (Ed.). *ALA World Encyclopedia of Library and Information Services* (pp. 634-36). 2nd edition. Chicago: American Library Association.

Ong, W. J. (1982). *Orality and Literacy: The Technologizing of the Word*. London: Methuen.

Oppenheim, C. (1993). "China's intellectual property rights and scientific and technical information services." *Aslib Proceedings*. 45, 261-6.

Orwell, G. (1946). *Charles Dickens*. In G. Orwell. *Dickens, Dali & Others* (pp. 1-75). New York: Harcourt Brace & World, Inc.

Ostler, L. J., T. C. Dahlin, and J. D. Willardson (1995). *The Closing of American Library Schools: Problems and Opportunities*. Westport, Conn.: Greenwood Press.

Oxford (1989). *The Oxford English Dictionary*. 2nd edition. Prepared by J. A. Simpson and E. S. C. Weiner. Oxford: Clarendon Press.

Patterson, L. R. (1968). *Copyright in Historical Perspective*. Nashville, Tenn.: Vanderbilt University Press.

Porter, G. (Ed.) (1980). *Encyclopedia of American Economic History*. New York: Charles Scribner's Sons.

Porty, C. R. (1977). The British experience 1876-1912: the impact of the telephone during the years of delay. In I. de Sola Pool (Ed.). *The Social Impact of the Telephone* (pp. 69-96). Cambridge, Mass.: MIT Press.

Proclamation. (1891). *By the President of the United States of America: A Proclamation*. July 1.

Proclamation. (1892a). *By the President of the United States of America: A Proclamation*. April 15.

Proclamation. (1892b). *By the President of the United States of America: A Proclamation*. October 31.

Ramsey, F. P. (1990). The foundations of mathematics. In D. H. Mellor (Ed.). *Philosophical Papers* (pp. 164-224). Cambridge, England: Cambridge University Press.

Rayward, W. B. (1999). "H. G. Wells's idea of a World Brain: a critical reassessment." *Journal of the American Society for Information Science*. 50, 557-73.

Reich, L. S. (1980). Science. In G. Porter (Ed.). *Encyclopedia of American Economic History* (pp. 281-93). New York: Charles Scribner's Sons.

Rijsbergen, C. J. van (1979). *Information Retrieval*. 2nd edition. London: Butterworths.

Ringer, B. (1985). The demonology of copyright. In B. H. Weil and B. F. Polansky (Eds.). *Modern Copyright Fundamentals: Key Writings on Technological and Other Issues* (pp. 24-28). New York: Van Nostrand Reinhold.

Roberts, N. (1976). "Social considerations towards a definition of information science." *Journal of Documentation*. 32, 249-57.

———. (1977). "Critique of the criteria." *Library Association Record*. 79, 556-557.

———. (1982). "A search for information man." *Social Science Information Studies*. 2, 93-104.

Rosenberg, N. (1976). *Perspectives on Technology*. Cambridge, England: Cambridge University Press, 1976.

———. (1980). Technology. In G. Porter (Ed.). *Encyclopedia of American Economic History* (pp. 294-308). New York: Charles Scribner's Sons.

———. (1982). *Inside the Black Box: Technology and Economics*. Cambridge, England: Cambridge University Press.

———. (1994). *Exploring the Black Box: Technology, Economics and History*. Cambridge, England: Cambridge University Press.

Rosenberg, V. (1974). "The scientific premises of information science." *Journal of the American Society for Information Science*. 25, 263-69.

Rothstein, M. (1980). Foreign trade. In G. Porter (Ed.). *Encyclopedia of American Economic History* (volume 1, pp. 247-63). New York: Charles Scribner's Sons.

Russell, B. (1920). *The Practice and Theory of Bolshevism*. London: Allen and Unwin.

Saracevic, T. (1976). "Relevance: a review of the literature and a framework for thinking on the notion in information science." *Advances in Librarianship*. 6, 79-138.

Saussure, F. de (1983). *Course in General Linguistics*. Edited by C. Bally and A. Sechehaye with the collaboration of A. Riedlinger, translated and annotated by R. Harris. London: Duckworth.

Sawyer Seminar. (2000). Computer Science as a Human Science: The Cultural Impact of Computerization, 1999-2000 Sawyer Seminar at the University of Chicago. At: http://humanities. uchicago.edu/ sawyer/CSasHS/. Last visited 28 August 2003.

Searle, J. R. (1980). "Minds, brains, and programs." *The Behavioral and Brain Sciences*. 3, 417-57.

Segal, H. P. (1993). Technology and social change. In M. K. Cayton, E. J. Gorn, and P. W. Williams (Eds.). *Encyclopedia of American Social History* (pp. 2297-322). New York: Charles Scribner's Sons.

Shakespeare, W. (1995). *Henry V* (The Arden Shakespeare). Edited by T. W. Craik. London: Routledge.

Shakespeare. (1984). *Macbeth* (The Arden Edition of the works of William Shakespeare). Edited by Kenneth Muir. London: Routledge.

Shannon, C. E. and W. Weaver (1949). *The Mathematical Theory of Communication*. : Urbana, Ill.: University of Illinois Press.

Shelley, M. (1998). *Frankenstein, or, The Modern Prometheus*. Oxford: Oxford University Press.

Shera, J. H. (1965a). Foundations of a theory of bibliography. In J. H. Shera, *Libraries and the Organization of Knowledge*. Edited by D. J. Foskett (pp. 18-33). Hamden, Conn.: Archon Books.

———. (1965b). Social epistemology, general semantics, and librarianship. In J. H. Shera. *Libraries and the Organization of Knowledge*. Edited by D. J. Foskett (pp. 12-17). Hamden, Conn.: Archon Books.

Skone James, F. E. (1948). *Copinger and Skone James on the Law of Copyright including International and Colonial Copyright, with the Statutes Relating Thereto and Forms and Precedents*. London: Sweet and Maxwell.

Smithson, S. (1994). "Information retrieval evaluation in practice: a case study approach." *Information Processing & Management*. 30, 205-221.

Sola Pool, I de (Ed.). (1977). *The Social Impact of the Telephone*. Cambridge, Mass.: MIT Press.

Solberg, T. (1939). *Copyright Miscellany: Being The Later Contributions Concerning the Protection of Literary and Artistic Property With Autobiographical Sketch, Portrait and Bibliography*. Boston, Mass.: John W. Luce and Company.

Stewart, J., and R. Williams (1998). "The coeveolution of society and multimedia technology: issues in predicting the future innovation and use of a ubiquitous technology." *Social Science Computer Review*. 16, 268-282.

Stieg, M. F. (1992). *Change and Challenge in Library and Information Science Education*. Chicago: American Library Association.

Stolpher, W. F. (1969). Schumpeter, Joseph A. In D. L. Sills (Ed.). *International Encyclopedia of the Social Sciences* (volume 14, 67-72). New York: Macmillan.

Swanson, D. R. (1988). "Historical note: information retrieval and the future of an illusion." *Journal of the American Society for Information Science*. 39, 92-98.

Swift, D. F., V. A. Winn, and D. A. Bramer (1977). "A multi-modal approach to indexing and classification." *International Classification*. 4, 90-94.

Thelin, J. R. (1993). The research university. In M. K. Cayton, E. J. Gorn, and P. W. Williams (Eds.). *Encyclopedia of American Social History* (pp. 2537-545). New York: Charles Scribner's Sons.

Transbinary Group. (1986). *Report of the Transbinary Group on Librarianship and Information Studies*. London: British Library.

Turner, F. J. (1996). The significance of the frontier in American history. In F. J. Turner. *The Frontier in American History* (pp. 1-38). New York: Dover Publications.

Twain, M. (1984). *Life on the Mississippi*. New York: Viking Penguin.

———. (1994). Fenimore Cooper's Literary Offenses. In M. Twain. *Tales, Speeches, Essays, and Sketches* (pp. 377-90). Harmondsworth, England: Penguin Books.

U. S. Congress. Office of Technology Assessment. (1986). *Intellectual Property Rights in an Age of Electronics and Information* (OTA-CIT-302). Washington, D.C.: Government Printing Office.

Vico, G. (1988). *On the Most Ancient Wisdom of the Italians: Unearthed from the Origins of the Latin Language: Including the Disputation with the Giornale De' Letterati d'Italia*. Translated. and introduced by L. M. Palmer. Ithaca, N.Y.: Cornell University Press.

———. (1976). *The New Science of Giambattista Vico*. Unabridged translation of the 3rd edition (1744) with the addition of "Practic of the New Science" by T. G. Bergin and M. H. Fisch. Ithaca, N.Y.: Cornell University Press.

Vološinov, V. N. (1986). *Marxism and the Philosophy of Language*. Cambridge, Mass.: Harvard University Press.

Walsham, G. (1998). "IT and changing professional identity: micro-studies and macro-theory." *Journal of the American Society for Information Science*. 49, 1081-89.

Warner, J. (1983). Liberalism and Marxism in the work of George Orwell. Ph.D. dissertation, Oxford University.

———. (1988). "British Library microform publications and their bibliographic control." *Journal of Librarianship*. 20, 159-80.

———. (1990). "Writing, literary work and document in United Kingdom copyright." *Journal of Information Science*. 16, 279-289.

———. (1991). "Writing, Programs, Computers and Logic." In Kevin P. Jones (Ed.). *Informatics 11: The Structuring of Information* (Proceedings of a conference held at the University of York, March 20-22, 1991) (pp. 109-45). London: Aslib.

———. (1992). "Retrieval performance tests in relation to online bibliographic searching." In D. Shaw (Ed.). *ASIS '92: Celebrating Change: Information Management on the Move* (Proceedings of the 55th ASIS Annual Meeting, Pittsburgh, Penn., 26-29, October 1992) (pp. 231-241). Medford, NJ: Learned Information for the American Society for Information Science.

———. (1993a). "Writing and literary work in copyright: a binational and historical analysis." *Journal of the American Society for Information Science*, 44, 307-21.

———. (1993b). "Review of M. Hancock-Beaulieu. *Information Systems for End Users: Research-and-Development Issues.*" *Journal of Documentation*. 49, 421-24.

———. (1994). *From Writing to Computers*. London: Routledge.

———. (1997). "The public reception of the Research Assessment Exercise 1996." *Aslib Proceedings*. 49, 263-76.

———. (1998a). "Review of B. Kahin and C. Nesson (Eds.). *Borders in Cyberspace: Information Policy and the Global Information Infrastructure.*" *Journal of the American Society for Information Science*. 49, 387-388.

———. (1998b). "Review of P. Levinson. *The Soft Edge: A Natural History and Future of the Information Revolution.*" *Journal of the American Society for Information Science*. 49, 1041.

———. (2001a). Not the exact words . . . : writing, computing, and exactness. In J. Warner. *Information, Knowledge, Text* (pp. 33-46). Lanham, M.D.: Scarecrow Press.

———. (2001b). Is there an origin to graphic communication? In J. Warner. *Information, Knowledge, Text* (pp. 105-9). Lanham, M.D.: Scarecrow Press.

———. (2001c). Shannon, Weaver, and the Minotaur. In: *Information, Knowledge, Text* (pp. 17-31). Lanham, M.D.: Scarecrow Press.

———. (2001d). Towards an integrated account of automata theory and formal logic: iconic and notational models. In J. Warner. *Information, Knowledge, Text* (pp. 47-72). Lanham, M.D.: Scarecrow Press.

Watson, L. E., and others (1973). "Sociology and information science." *Journal of Librarianship*. 5, 270-83.

Webster, F. (1995a). *Theories of the Information Society*. London: Routledge.

———. (1995b). "Review of John Feather. *The Information Society: A Study of Continuity and Change.*" *Journal of Librarianship and Information Science*. 27, 175-76.

Wells, H. G. (1902). *Anticipations of The Reaction of Mechanical and Scientific Progress on Human Life and Thought*. London: Chapman and Hall.

White, H. D., and K. W. McCain (1998). "Visualizing a discipline: an author co-citation analysis of information science, 1972-1995." *Journal of the American Society for Information Science*. 49, 327-55.

White, R. (1994). Frederick Jackson Turner and Buffalo Bill. In J. R. Grossman (Ed.). *The Frontier in American Culture* (An exhibition at the Newberry Library, August 26, 1994 - January 7, 1995) (pp.7-65). Los Angeles, Calif.: University of California Press.

Whitehead, A. N., and B. Russell. (1962). *Principia Mathematica to *56*. 2nd edition. Cambridge, England: Cambridge University Press.

Wiener, N. (1954). *The Human Use of Human Beings: Cybernetics and Society*. New York: De Capo Press.

———. (1993). *Invention: The Care and Feeding of Ideas*. Cambridge, Mass.: MIT Press.

Wilson, P. (1973). "Situational relevance." *Information Storage and Retrieval*. 9, 457-471 .

———. (1983). *Second-Hand Knowledge: An Enquiry into Cognitive Authority* (Contributions in Librarianship and Information Science 44). Westport, Conn.: Greenwood Press.

———. (1990). "Copyright, derivative rights, and the first amendment." *Library Trends*. 39, 92-110.

———. (1993). "Review of Margaret F. Stieg. *Change and Challenge in Library and Information Science Education*." *College and Research Libraries*. 54, 275-76.

———. (1996a). Some consequences of information overload and rapid conceptual change. In J. Olaisen, E. Munch-Petersen, and P. Wilson (Eds.). *Information Science: From the Development of the Discipline to Social Interaction* (pp. 21-34). Oslo: Scandinavian University Press.

———. (1996b). "Review of Larry J. Ostler, Therrin C. Dahlin, and J. D. Willardson. *The Closing of American Library Schools: Problems and Opportunities*." *College and Research Libraries*. 57, 197-98.

———. (1996c). The future of research in our field. In J. Olaisen, E. Munch-Petersen, and P. Wilson (Eds.). *Information Science: From the Development of the Discipline to Social Interaction*. Oslo: Scandinavian University Press.

———. (2000). "Review of Allan Pratt. *The Information of the Image*. 2nd Edition." *The Library Quarterly*. 70, 135-137.

Wilson, T. D. (2000). Curriculum and catastrophe: change in professional education. Paper presented at ALISE 2000 Annual Conference, San Antonio, Texas, January 11-14, 2000. Website http://www. alise. org/nondiscuss/conf00 Wilson-Curriculum. htm (last accessed June 3, 2000).

Winner, L. (1977). *Autonomous Technology: Technics-Out-Of-Control as a Theme in Political Thought*. Cambridge, Mass.: MIT Press.

Wittgenstein, L. (1981). *Tractatus Logico-Philosophicus*. London: Routledge and Kegan Paul.

Wood, K. (1992). Education and training. In D. Bromley and A. M. Allott (Eds.). *British Librarianship and Information Work 1986-1990. Volume 1. General Libraries and the Profession* (pp. 208-19). London: Library Association.

Wyn, E., and J. L. Katz (1997). "Hyperbole over cyberspace: self-presentation and social boundaries in Internet home pages and discourse." *Information Society*. 13, 297-327.

Yuengling Jr. v. Schile. (1882). *Yuengling Jr. v. Schile*. Circuit Court, S. D. New York – April 3, 1882. In *Decisions of the United States Courts Involving Copyright and Literary Property* (Copyright Office Bulletin No. 15) (pp. 3033-42). Washington, D.C.: Copyright Office, Library of Congress, 1909.

Index

About the Author

Julian Warner is a faculty member in the School of Management and Economics, The Queen's University of Belfast.

He was a visiting scholar at the School of Library and Information Studies, University of California at Berkeley 1991-1992 and at the Graduate School of Library and Information Science, University of Illinois 2000.

His previous publications include *From Writing to Computers*. London: Routledge, 1994, and *Information, Knowledge, Text*. Lanham, M.D.: Scarecrow Press, 2001.

www.ingramcontent.com/pod-product-compliance
Ingram Content Group UK Ltd.
Pitfield, Milton Keynes, MK11 3LW, UK
UKHW021034150926
475561UK00003B/93

9 780810 849563